FOUR FLORIDA MODERNS

FOUR FLORIDA MODERNS

THE ARCHITECTURE OF ALBERTO ALFONSO, RENÉ GONZÁLEZ, CHAD OPPENHEIM & GUY W. PETERSON

With contributions by Robert McCarter, Charles Gwathmey, Richard Meier, Terence Riley & Warren R. Schwartz

Saxon Henry

W. W. Norton & Company
New York • London

TITLE PAGE: ECHOING LE CORBUSIER'S USE OF "BRUTE CONCRETE," PETERSON
CHOSE TO LEAVE THE EXTERNAL FRAME OF THE FREUND RESIDENCE
UNFINISHED. THE ROUGHNESS OF ITS SURFACE BECOMES A CONTRASTING
ELEMENT TO THE COLORFUL CUBES THE FRAME ENVELOPES.

FOR INFORMATION ABOUT PERMISSION TO REPRODUCE SELECTIONS FROM THIS BOOK,
WRITE TO PERMISSIONS, W. W. NORTON & COMPANY, INC., 500 FIFTH AVENUE, NEW YORK, NY 10110

FOR INFORMATION ABOUT SPECIAL DISCOUNTS FOR BULK PURCHASES, PLEASE CONTACT
W. W. NORTON SPECIAL SALES AT SPECIALSALES@WWNORTON.COM OR 800-233-4830.

BOOK DESIGN BY MATTHEW BOULOUTIAN & VIVIAN GHAZARIAN, MODERN GOOD
MANUFACTURING BY KHL PRINTING COMPANY
PRODUCTION MANAGER: LEEANN GRAHAM

LIBRARY OF CONGRESS CATALOGING-IN-PUBLICATION DATA

HENRY, SAXON.
  FOUR FLORIDA MODERNS : THE ARCHITECTURE OF ALBERTO E. ALFONSO, RENÉ GONZÁLEZ,
CHAD OPPENHEIM, & GUY PETERSON / SAXON HENRY.
    P. CM.
  INCLUDES BIBLIOGRAPHICAL REFERENCES AND INDEX.
  ISBN 978-0-393-73274-0 (HARDCOVER)
1. ARCHITECTURE--FLORIDA--HISTORY--20TH CENTURY. 2. ARCHITECTURE--FLORIDA--HISTORY--21ST CENTURY.
3. MODERN MOVEMENT (ARCHITECTURE)--INFLUENCE. I. TITLE. II. TITLE: ARCHITECTURE OF
ALBERTO E. ALFONSO, RENÉ GONZÁLEZ, CHAD OPPENHEIM, & GUY PETERSON.

NA730.F6H46 2009
720.9759--DC22

                          2009005808

ISBN 13: 978-0-393-73274-0

W. W. NORTON & COMPANY, INC., 500 FIFTH AVENUE, NEW YORK, N.Y. 10110
WWW.WWNORTON.COM
W. W. NORTON & COMPANY LTD., CASTLE HOUSE, 75/76 WELLS ST., LONDON W1T 3QT
1 2 3 4 5 6 7 8 9 0

With thanks to Nancy Green at W. W. Norton & Company for her faith in this project. Thanks also to the architects who took time from their incredibly busy lives to write analyses of the works presented in this book. Thanks to artist Alejandro Vigilante for helping me to select photography from such a wealth of material that it was difficult to narrow down the choices. A special thanks to Joe Spinelli, who has a keen eye when editing textual material. Thanks also to Donald Singer, FAIA, John Howey, FAIA, Ana Gonzalez at the Historical Museum of Southern Florida, and Bunny and William Morgan for their efforts in helping me to secure historical photography.

ALBERTO ALFONSO, AIA

RENÉ GONZÁLEZ, AIA

CHAD OPPENHEIM, NCARB, AIA

GUY W. PETERSON, NCARB, FAIA

THE **MODERN** IS NOT A STYLE

Florida's Other Tradition of Architecture

→ PAUL RUDOLPH MADE A REMARKABLE CONTRIBUTION TO FLORIDA'S MODERN ARCHITECTURAL HERITAGE WITH BUILDINGS LIKE HIS RIVERVIEW HIGH SCHOOL IN SARASOTA.

→→ FRANK LLOYD WRIGHT'S ANNIE PFEIFFER CHAPEL, ON THE CAMPUS OF FLORIDA SOUTHERN COLLEGE, WAS BUILT BETWEEN 1939 AND 1941 WITH THE HELP OF STUDENT LABOR.

Modern architecture is alive and well and living in Florida. The work of the four architects documented in this book, representatives of the current generation of modern architects in Florida, should serve notice that, to paraphrase Mark Twain, the rumors of the demise of modernism have been greatly exaggerated. For the last hundred years, and through several generations, the works of the best Florida practitioners have exemplified modern architecture's characteristics of engagement and enhancement of the environment, forthright expression of construction and authenticity of materials, ability to house new and differing lifestyles, spatial freedom combined with a sense of place, and reinforcement of our identity as those who in fact live in the modern age.

In these works, modern architecture is shown to be uniquely capable of making places where contemporary cultural, social, and domestic aspirations are realized in harmony with the climate, topography, and environment of Florida. Yet modern architecture, like all living traditions, cannot survive without our individual experiences of its spaces—without our lives literally "taking place" within it. In other words, as a construction rooted in its particular time and place, modern architecture is not a style.

Modern architecture could be said to have first arrived in Florida with the young Bernard Maybeck—famous for his later works in California—who was the construction architect for Carrère and Hastings' Ponce de Leon and Alcazar Hotels, built in St. Augustine in 1885–86. Rather than the design of the buildings, it was their innovative construction, including the deployment of cast concrete, which incorporates local coral stone as aggregate, and the use of iron railroad rails as a kind of primitive reinforcement over openings, that marks these works as modern. The adaptation of new universal construction techniques to regional traditions of building and locally available materials is perhaps the

most important constant we can follow through the works of succeeding generations of Florida modern architects.

While not well known, the next examples of this modern tradition are the 1910–20 works of John Klutho in Jacksonville, and Antonin Nichodema in Tampa and Puerto Rico, both of whom were directly inspired by the Prairie Period works of Frank Lloyd Wright. Wright himself brought his interpretation of modern architecture to Florida in the late 1930s when he began work on what would eventually be the largest collection of his buildings anywhere in the world, Florida Southern College in Lakeland. Wright's designs, which received the widest possible publicity, predated and paralleled the arrival of the Art Moderne–style hotels to Miami Beach, and they had a far greater impact on the evolution of modern architecture in Florida.

Contemporary with Fallingwater, the Johnson Wax Building, Taliesin West, and the first of the Usonian Houses,

the buildings of Florida Southern College were markedly different from these other works by Wright, in particular in the manner in which he used two scales of concrete to respond to the landscape of existing citrus orchards. Near the ground, and close to where people walked in the shade of the trees and his canopies, Wright designed walls that were made of small-scale, custom-designed concrete blocks, intricately detailed, with colored glass insets. Above the trees, and only visible from a distance, Wright designed walls made of large-scale, smooth, monolithic cast concrete, which stood and shone in the strong Florida sunlight.

Despite Wright's consistent efforts to adapt his designs to local conditions, in the years immediately following World War II International Style architecture appeared to have achieved universal dominance, its standardized formula intended to be the same around the world. Yet it is hardly coincidental that, exactly at this moment of universal stylistic unification, several important outbreaks of regional architectural character were also taking place, including the Bay Area School in San Francisco, the Case Study Houses in Los Angeles, and the Sarasota School in Florida. Contrary to its universal aspirations, articulated in the 1932 Museum of Modern Art "International Style" exhibit, the constructed embodiment of modern architectural principles seemed to require their being grounded in the unique characteristics of a particular place and time.

Wright's ongoing work in Lakeland both served as an inspiration for those young architects already living in Florida, including Rufus Nims and Alfred Browning Parker, and drew a new generation of young architects to the state, most notably Paul Rudolph. In Sarasota, Rudolph became the most famous of a group of architects whose wide variety of designs within such a small community defied the stereotypical representation of modern architecture as lacking richness and diversity. Like many of the regional modernist movements of 1945–65, the Sarasota architects did not see themselves as unified in their interpretation of modern architecture, and the remarkable diversity of the designs of architects such as Ralph Twitchell, Victor Lundy, Tim Seibert, Mark Hampton, Gene Leedy, Carl Abbott, and others bears this out.

For architects from around the world searching for alternatives to the universal formula of the International Style, the work of the Sarasota School came as a revelation, embodying an entirely new vision of the relation of modern architecture to its place. Today the concept of critical regionalism, first articulated by Wright disciple Harwell Hamilton Harris in 1954 and later championed by the most important architectural historian of our time, Kenneth Frampton, calls for exactly this kind of regionally inflected modern architecture, true to the universal intentions of spatial liberation, yet capable of engaging local climate, landscape, building traditions, and materials.

Florida was also home to other, heretofore less recognized, regional "schools" of modern architecture, most notably the architects who realized a series of remarkable works in the Miami area following World War II. This group,

↓ ALFRED BROWNING PARKER DESIGNED THIS RESIDENCE IN MIAMI FOR HIM-SELF. FRANK LLOYD WRIGHT DEEMED IT ORGANIC ARCHITECTURE AT ITS BEST.

↑ IGOR POLEVITZKY'S BIRDCAGE HOUSE IN MIAMI BEACH IS APTLY NAMED FOR ITS DOMINANT SCREENED PATIO THAT GREATLY EXPANDED THE LIVING SPACES OF THE HOME.

which I have called the tropical modern school, includes both the Wright-inspired works of Robert Bradford Browne, George Reed, and Parker—one of the very few architects about whom Wright had kind words to say, as evidenced by his praise of Parker's own house of 1952—as well as the more minimalist works of Nims, Robert Weed, and Igor Polevitzky.

After designing such extraordinary works as the Deering Residence and the Riverview High School, Rudolph left Florida to become dean at Yale in 1958, and the Sarasota School dispersed soon after. Yet Rudolph would exert one last influence over the next generation when he hired the young Floridian Robert Ernest, a recent graduate of Yale and former student there of Louis I. Kahn, to oversee construction of his Milam House in Ponte Vedra (1959–61). This house, with its famous monumental sun-screen facing the ocean, is built with concrete blocks, those cast-offs of the construction industry that Wright had been endeavoring to ennoble since the early 1920s. Ernest, who died of cancer at age twenty-nine in 1962, realized only three built works of his own design—the Ernest House, a tropical interpretation of Le Corbusier's interlocking section; the Becker House, with its unique rhomboid-shaped concrete blocks and Wrightian hexagonal planning grid; and the Northside Youth Center, with its innovative, Kahn-inspired folded plate concrete roof—all in Jacksonville.

Despite being so few in number, the elegant concrete block wall construction of Ernest's works inspired what I have called the concrete block school in Florida. Among its members, many of whom are still practicing today, are Dan Duckham; Lowell Lotspeich; Robert Broward, whose Wright-inspired designs reveal his early training as a Wright apprentice at Taliesin; Donald Singer, whose Kahn-inspired concrete places stand stoically silent in the landscape of illusions which Florida is fast becoming; and William Morgan, who in his fifty-year career has developed three modern construction types—earth, tree, and tower buildings—that engage modern architecture in the landscape and climate of Florida, unfolding for today the implications of his explorations of ancient earth-mound structures in the Americas.

↓ THE DEERING HOUSE ON CASEY KEY, ONE OF PAUL RUDOLPH'S SARASOTA SCHOOL RESIDENCES, ILLUSTRATES HOW A FASCINATION WITH NATURAL LIGHT'S INFLUENCES UPON INTERIOR ARCHITECTURE WAS A SARASOTA SCHOOL TENET.

↑ PAUL RUDOLPH'S MILAM HOUSE, WITH ITS MONUMENTAL SUN-SCREEN, IS BUILT OF CONCRETE BLOCK, THE CAST-OFFS OF THE CONSTRUCTION INDUSTRY.

A consistent characteristic common to these diverse architects, which continues today in the best practices, is the sense of modern architecture as a living tradition. That is, modern architecture practiced as a way of designing and building that, from generation to generation, shares not a fixed style or set of forms, but the same fundamental ordering principles. Primary among these are minimizing energy, material, and damage to the environment while maximizing the richness of the experiences of the inhabitants, the accommodation of a lifestyle appropriate to the tropics, and the engagement of each building with its natural environment and climate.

As an example, all of the buildings I have mentioned were designed to do without air-conditioning by engaging prevailing breezes and employing sun-shading, and to nestle into their sites, adjusting themselves to the surrounding nature without in any way imitating it. This sense of economy, of gaining the maximum benefit for the inhabitants in terms of the enrichment of the daily rituals of life, over the lifetime of a building, from the least energy and material investment, has always been part of the best modern architecture. In fact, it was an ethical imperative for architects such as Wright and those he inspired. Following this tradition, the work illustrated here, like the best architecture around the world, is defined first and foremost by the quality of our experience of inhabiting it.

Which brings us to the contemporary moment in Florida, and the superficial conceptions of architecture, entirely disengaged from any real place, that dominate the society in which the works presented in this book are being built. Today modern architecture is most often characterized not as a living, ever-transforming, contemporary tradition, but rather as yet another style available for selection by the eclectic designer, alongside the various so-called historical or traditional styles fashionable at any given moment. What is today called "traditional" architecture in Florida presents on its exterior a thin veneer of some cannibalized "style"— the so-called Mediterranean revival is the most popular at the moment—which is in fact nothing historical at all, not having existed prior to its contemporary concoction. This "traditional" exterior styling exhibits a kind of schizophrenia, for, while purportedly providing curb appeal when seen from the outside, it is in fact totally divorced from the thoroughly modern life that takes place within it, as well as from its place, Florida.

This disengagement from the particularities of Florida as a tropical place is exemplified by the dependence on air-conditioning in these so-called traditional buildings, largely because they fail to employ such place-determining and experientially beneficial aspects as solar orientation, shading, and prevailing breezes, while at the same time they eradicate existing vegetation, replacing it with lawns and "landscaping." Far more important than the fact that they are not sustainable by any definition of the word, these buildings deny their unfortunate occupants any sensory engagement of their environment. It is clear that these so-called traditional buildings could in fact be constructed anywhere, and thus those inhabiting them are, quite literally, nowhere.

Standing directly opposite this depressing trend is the modern architecture of Florida, as exemplified by the works of these four practices. While today it often seems that what a building looks like from the outside is all that matters, these four architects and their peers know that it is what a building is like to live in that makes it truly modern. The need for adaptations of modern architecture's universal liberative spatial concepts to local culture, climate, and landscape—and the parallel integration of innovative and traditional construction technologies and materials—is perhaps more pressing today than ever before.

In this, the works of modern architecture in Florida, in both its historical and contemporary manifestations, demonstrate the significant benefits of an evolutionary, rather than revolutionary, development of architecture. It could be argued that modern architecture survives today only through the embodiment of its principles in the works of regional groups of architects, such as the examples presented in this book. Understood as a living tradition, modern architecture is not a style to be either cataloged or copied, but rather a discipline to be practiced. Only through its engagement with reality—revealed in our experience of inhabiting its spaces—is modern architecture grounded, transformed, and reborn in any given time and place.

Robert McCarter
RUTH AND NORMAN MOORE PROFESSOR OF ARCHITECTURE, WASHINGTON UNIVERSITY, ST. LOUIS

↑ A CLEVER CANTILEVERED CONCRETE SLAB SERVES AS A LIGHT FIXTURE ABOVE THE DINING TABLE OF THE BRODY RESIDENCE IN MIAMI, DESIGNED BY DONALD SINGER.

↓ WILLIAM MORGAN'S HILLTOP HOUSE IN GAINESVILLE IS ONE OF THE ARCHITECT'S "EARTH" STRUCTURES.

PROFOUND ECHOES

Creatively, Alberto Alfonso, René González, Chad Oppenheim, and Guy Peterson—the four Florida architects presented in this book—are more different than similar, but
the philosophical principles they adhere to bind them to the
historical trajectory of modernism. In what has become an
impassioned calling, their embrace of modernism reflects
four very unique aesthetic approaches, which are carefully
detailed and revealed in the pages that follow.

While the types of buildings they design span the
spectrum from airports, medical facilities, and museums
to open-air chapels, waterfront homes, and condominium
complexes, the four Florida moderns share an architectural language that had its first utterances in Peter Behrens's
Berlin studio between 1907 and 1911, when modernism's
greats—Walter Gropius, Ludwig Mies van der Rohe, and Le
Corbusier—apprenticed there.

Le Corbusier collected his early writings on modernism
in his groundbreaking book *Vers une architecture*, first published in 1923 and translated into English in 1927. In this
manifesto, an important catalyst for these four architects, Corb
states, "Passion can create drama out of inert stone."[1] Not only
did the philosophies of the early modernists like Corb, Mies,
and Gropius ignite passions in these Florida moderns when
they were students, but their ideas spurred their pilgrimages,

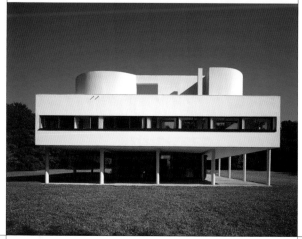

→ THE ANNIE PFEIFFER CHAPEL AT FLORIDA SOUTHERN COLLEGE IN LAKELAND,
DESIGNED BY FRANK LLOYD WRIGHT, IS ONE OF FLORIDA'S EARLIEST
MODERNIST GEMS.

→ THE VILLA SAVOYE IN POISSY, FRANCE (1928), WHICH WAS DESIGNED
BY LE CORBUSIER, IS STILL AN IMPORTANT MODERNIST STRUCTURE MORE
THAN THREE-QUARTERS OF A CENTURY AFTER IT WAS BUILT.

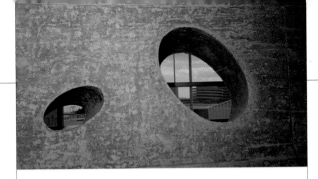

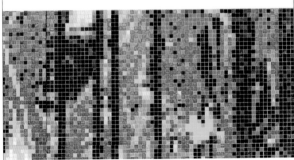

drove the development of their design aesthetic, and still figure significantly in their tenets as educators.

The trajectory of modernism extends from these early moderns to the mentors and teachers of the four Florida architects presented in this book—including the late Charles Gwathmey, Richard Meier, Terence Riley, and Warren Schwartz, who offer insightful analyses of the work of their younger colleagues. As the four continue to make significant marks on Florida's urbanscapes and rural settings, Alfonso, González, Oppenheim, and Peterson consider themselves to be among the current generation of modernists to bring the vernacular forward in Florida.

Their participation in this thriving movement of regional Florida modernism is explored in this book through an introduction that provides a snapshot of each architect's journey to modernism, an analysis of each architect's work by an architectural leader whose work was so influential to his own, a process interview, and a selection of the architect's commissions illustrated with photographs, sketches, and drawings.

The four architects featured here further modernism's march into the future. Alfonso, González, Oppenheim, and

← ALBERTO ALFONSO'S ARCHITECTURE, AS THESE OCULAR PUNCTURES IN THE FACADE OF AIRSIDE C AT THE TAMPA INTERNATIONAL AIRPORT SHOW, DISPLAYS AN UNCOMPROMISING ATTENTION TO DETAIL.

← THE NEW YORK FIVE [CHARLES GWATHMEY, RICHARD MEIER, PETER EISENMAN, MICHAEL GRAVES, AND JOHN HEJDUK] WERE CHAMPIONING A RETURN TO THE MODERNISM TYPIFIED BY LUDWIG MIES VAN DER ROHE, WHOSE FARNSWORTH HOUSE IS LAUDED AS A MODERNIST TREASURE.

← MEIER SAYS OF THIS PROJECT BY GONZÁLEZ, THE CISNEROS FONTANALS ART FOUNDATION, THAT "MAN-MADE ELEMENTS OF CONCRETE, METAL, TILE, AND STONE ARE EMBEDDED WITHIN THE JUNGLE CONTEXT."

← WALTER GROPIUS, WHO WOULD FOUND THE STAATLICHES BAUHAUS IN 1919 IN WEIMAR, GERMANY, DESIGNED HIS HOME IN LINCOLN, MASSACHU-SETTS, IN THE SPIRIT OF THE AGE OF MODERNISM.

Peterson speak of the intuitive, the unfolding of spatial experience, the sensory aspects of architecture, and the enhancement of the human condition. These preoccupations inspire them to plumb the depths of their collective calling as they strive to emulate Le Corbusier's desire to create an architecture that awakens "profound echoes" in humanity.[2]

Indeed, each architect examined feels his architectural and philosophical heritage acutely, a legacy that, in speaking with me for this book, Alfonso acknowledges: "Corb, Mies and, later, the New York Five [Charles Gwathmey, Richard Meier, Peter Eisenman, Michael Graves, and John Hejduk were grappling with huge ideas in their time in order to further develop this ethic that we now call modernism. We are the benefactors of these previous investigations, which have played a significant role in creating a new construct that we can call our own and develop, even as we are grounded in our particular time and place."

↑ PETERSON'S RICH ARCHITECTURAL VISION INCLUDES EXPERIENTIAL MOMENTS, AS IN THIS RESIDENCE ON BIRD KEY.

↑ THIS VIEW OF WILLIAM MORGAN'S HILLTOP HOUSE IN GAINESVILLE ILLUSTRATES THE HERITAGE THAT EARLY FLORIDA MODERNS WERE BUILDING FOR THE GENERATIONS TO COME.

↑ CHAD OPPENHEIM'S ARCHITECTURE, WHICH TERENCE RILEY DEEMS AN ARCHITECTURE OF DUALITY, MAKES A VIVID STATEMENT AS IT INTERACTS WITH THE STRONG SOUTH FLORIDA LIGHT.

ALBERTO ALFONSO, AIA

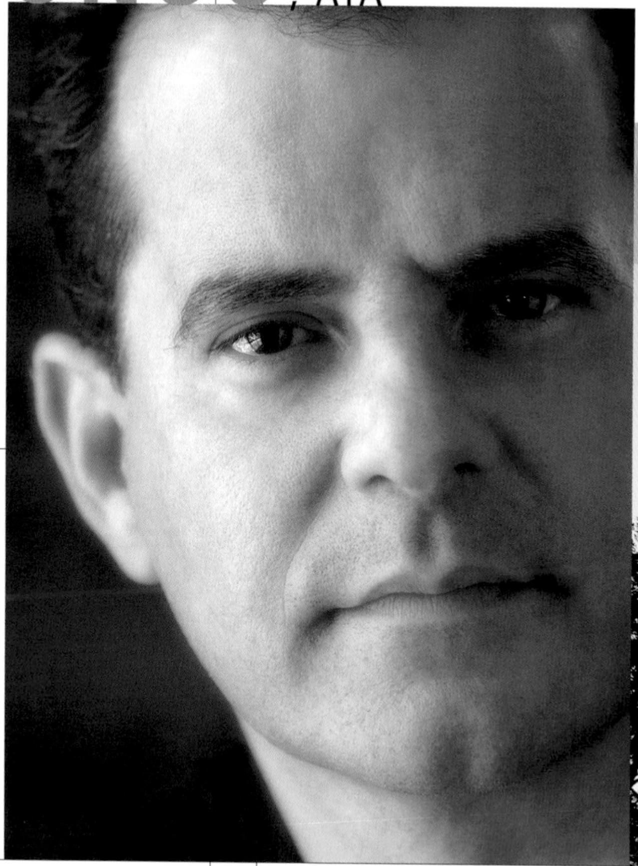

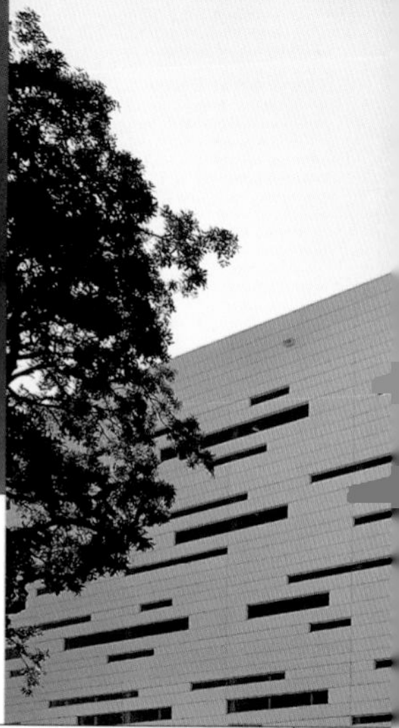

Alfonso Architects | Tampa, Florida

"I was fortunate to have been raised in the house of an architect," remarks Alberto Alfonso, son of the late Carlos Alfonso Sr., who was a forward-thinking modernist during the 1950s.

While building a practice in Havana and teaching architecture at the University of Havana, Carlos Sr. grew weary of the Beaux Arts–driven curriculum there, so much so that he invited Walter Gropius to the university to speak about the International Style of architecture. "That single event was no doubt instrumental in the purification of Cuban architecture, which led to the creation of a Cuban modernism," says Alberto.

Though his father's practice was thriving in Havana, Fidel Castro's policies were becoming threatening. When the regime strengthened, moving toward a flashpoint, the elder Alfonso felt that it was necessary to remove his family from the country, out of harm's way. "Dad was designing a high-rise for Castro, which gave him an insider's glimpse as to what was truly happening," Alberto recalls. "His impulse to get us out proved to be incredibly wise."

Alberto was two years old when his family arrived in Florida in 1960. He recalls that his father's love for his profession made such an indelible impression on him that following his lead was a natural choice. "His heroes became my heroes: Eames, Corb, Rudolph, Kahn." Alberto attended the University of Florida School of Architecture to obtain undergraduate and graduate degrees. Early in his education, he participated in visiting studio classes led by Charles Gwathmey and Richard Meier. Just as his father's artistry had, Gwathmey's concepts made a lasting impression on him. Each of these influential architects instilled in him the notion that architecture is, first and foremost, about building a consistent body of work.

"When I am designing, I consider the questions that hover in my subconscious: 'How would Dad approach this? What would Charlie say about this? Would they ask if I am compromising?'" he explains. "I believe those echoes are important if we are to hold ourselves to a standard of producing exemplary architecture." Alberto earned his graduate degree in 1983, and along with classmate Angel del Monte, joined the firm founded by his father and his brother, Carlos Alfonso Jr., who is also an architect.

As he has participated in building the firm to its current stature, Alberto's creative process, which is continually influenced by music, film, and art, has informed the projects designed by Alfonso Architects. "The ability of

↑ ALBERTO ALFONSO'S FATHER, CARLOS, WAS BUILDING A SUBSTANTIVE BODY OF WORK IN HAVANA, CUBA, UNTIL POLITICAL UNREST PROPELLED HIM OUT OF THE COUNTRY.

phenomena that are outside the normal realm of architectural problem solving to inform our work is of great interest to me," he remarks. This means that when Alfonso begins his search for the soul of a project, it may start with a painting or a piece of music or the way light filters across a wall at a particular time of day.

Subscribing to the ideals Le Corbusier expressed in *Creation is a Patient Search*, Alberto will design as far into the process as will allow for change. This helps him and his design team to produce an architecture that is highly personal. "We do not perceive modernism as a style, but as a process," says Alberto, who believes that one of Le Corbusier's great legacies is a truthful approach to architecture. "Our work tries to be tectonic in its honesty of expression, which means we don't do dishonest things," he adds. "The struggle is in the editing. When is the curve the right curve? When is too much too much? The answer is that it just has to feel right."

Alfonso's resolve to create a body of work that embodies a linear thought process is paramount. "There is a rational aspect, or glue, that holds our work together," he states. "But we also aim to couple that with the intuitive, poetic side, which we believe gives the work its richness. To deliberately repeat our ideas for the sake of creating a vocabulary would become mundane." Alfonso embraces a Kahn precept—that architecture should incorporate the measurable and the unmeasurable; that the architect is both poet and scientist. Addressing the unmeasurable prevents Alfonso from falling into the trap of creating buildings without that soulful element he sees as critical to memorable architecture.

ANALYSIS **by Charles Gwathmey, FAIA, principal of Gwathmey Siegel & Associates Architects, New York City**

Architecture is evolutionary. We are being constantly provoked and challenged by issues and ideas that provide opportunities to extend and explore, as well as to reevaluate. The critical creative test is that one must continue to take risks, to determine both validity and durability, literally and philosophically. Or, to paraphrase Picasso, "If you know exactly what you are going to do, what is the point of doing it?"

Alberto Alfonso was once my student at the University of Florida, and I knew then that he would contribute and prevail as an architect of substance. His passion was obvious, his work ethic was uncompromised, his curiosity was unhesitating, and his values were uncontaminated. We have remained friends and colleagues over the years, and when asked to write this essay I was honored and flattered. I am not a critic, but a critical observer who understands the discovery process and the struggle to realization.

Alberto was clearly inspired and motivated by the work of his father, the Cuban architect Carlos Alfonso, whose early modernist, Bauhaus-influenced buildings resonated with a structural and geometric clarity as well as a vernacular overlay that referenced the cultural and environmental specifics of place.

Despite the fact that all of the Alfonso projects are in Florida, there is a formal construct, a disciplined analytical process, and a universality that separates the work from vernacular dependence. The body of work is extensive and incredibly varied. It is simultaneously rational and romantic,

↑ LAKE HOUSE #1 IN TAMPA, DESIGNED BY ALFONSO, IS
SCULPTURALLY DYNAMIC AND VOLUMETRICALLY RICH.

rigorous and poetic, responsive and interpretive, holistic and visionary. No matter the specifics of each project, the ethic is consistent.

The Mission of St. Mary open-air chapel in Tampa—a low-budget, outdoor pavilion that establishes a spiritual sense of place through its minimal essentialness and tectonic clarity—is a strategic and transforming realization. The articulate structure, the sequential hierarchal circulation that fulfills the expectation, the serenity of the "chapel" enclosed by the floating asymmetrical curved wall, the extension of the space to the garden offer a totality and summary of problem solving through invention and sensitivity

↓ THE STRUCTURE OF ST. MARY'S HAS A TECTONIC CLARITY AND A MINIMAL ESSENTIALNESS.

that makes architecture inspiring. It is also a confirmation of Alfonso's choice of Michael Leyton's dictum: "Asymmetry is the memory that processes leave on objects / symmetry is the absence of process—memory."[1]

Lake House #1 (2006) extends the material palette, program complexity, and compositional collage to a refined level of resolution, one that is hierarchally clear, sculpturally dynamic, and volumetrically rich. Lake House #2 (2007) is at this time in Alfonso's discovery process the most romantic and form/sculptural intuitive project to date. It is a summary of "modern architecture" from Le Corbusier's Chandigarh to Firminy, Bauhaus to Gehry, and even Diller + Scofidio. The enthusiasm and energy afforded by this opportunity is explosive, and in a true sense encompasses the oeuvre to date. The question is, how will he edit?

I will close with the Tampa International Airport project, which I toured a year ago without preconceptions or expectations. Given the restrictions, programmatic complexities, circulation separations, systems integration, and scale and volumetric opportunities, the airport is a prized architectural commission. How many airports are memorable? Most are repetitive exposed structural articulations that in the end fade. Tampa's Airside C is an exception: asymmetrical, organic, spatially sensuous, volumetrically dynamic, and materially dense.

The anticipation begins at the tram's arrival into a poured concrete, abstractly fenestrated space, opening into the plan-rotated security zone, which is articulated by clerestory backlighting, a sloped ceiling, and curved wood object walls separating the initial waiting spaces—all extended by complex sectional manipulations that articulate circulation and waiting areas. The oval plan extends the expectation by

↑ A MODEL FOR LAKE HOUSE #2, WHICH CHARLES GWATHMEY DEEMS
ALFONSO'S MOST INTUITIVE PROJECT TO DATE.

sequentially revealing the spaces while simultaneously affording a sense of intimacy, sensuality, and variation that is atypical. The similarity to St. Mary's Chapel is refreshing and undeniable. One should fly to Tampa to experience a unique and aspirational, transforming architecture.

In all the projects, despite the constraints of program, budget, and site, the level of resolution and refinement is consistent, as is the frustration of limitations. The idea that out of constraints comes invention is confirmed, and separates the work from the conventional to the art of architecture. I am a proud admirer of Alfonso Architects and do not mind reversing roles, from teacher to student.

ON PROCESS **A Conversation with Alberto Alfonso**

Saxon Henry: How does your creative process show itself with each new project?

As a student, I made a pilgrimage to Le Corbusier's Ronchamp, where I found a tiny book containing his texts about and sketches of Ronchamp. One passage always resonates with me when I begin a project. He wrote that when a job was handed to him, he tucked it away in his memory, not even making sketches for months on end. He felt that the human head was made to have a certain independence— he actually called it a box into which you can toss the elements of a problem and leave them to float and to ferment. Suddenly there would come a spontaneous movement from within: a catch is sprung and that's the time to take a pencil or a drawing charcoal or some colored pencils and give birth on a sheet of paper.

This is important because the temptation is to grab a program and jump right into the design process, immediately trying to solve some of the physical components of the rooms, the adjacencies and the square footages—solving the pragmatics of the building.

Kahn writes about an architecture that incorporates the measurable and the unmeasurable, declaring the architect to be both poet and scientist. We see this unmeasurable aspect as the form-giver. The trap of simply following a vocabulary without giving a building a soul produces architecture that is lacking. If we were only creating buildings to solve programs or to simply follow an established architectonic language, I would have been bored with that long ago. If we can come up with an essence, one that we can always reference, then we have something.

Can you give a few examples of this from your projects?

With Airside C at the Tampa International Airport, I reminisced about flying during the time when I was a child, when flying was a privilege. Passengers would dress up for the occasion, the stewardesses were hip, and the pilots were

↓ AIRSIDE C AT THE TAMPA INTERNATIONAL AIRPORT.

the rock stars of the time. There was an incredible anticipation and jet flight was a new experience.

During that period, my dad was working on the design of the Tampa International Airport. He embarked on a tour in 1964 to study other airports, a trip during which he took photographs. I remember sitting in the living room as he showed us slides of Saarinen's TWA terminal and the Dulles terminal. Even at that age, I recognized how those buildings celebrated the idea of flight. These memories became a reference for the project.

Because the Sam Rampello School's curriculum focuses heavily on the musical arts, I collaborated with a composer to write a piece of music about the journey of education. The music inspired the layering and graphic language we used in the project. Also, because the school is nestled into a harsh urban environment, the site naturally influenced the building's desire to be a shelter; it demanded that the building be a refuge with an inside core to protect the children within it. Combining this with the music created layers of meaning, which made the design of the building richer. I had read that Corb dabbled with this idea of musicality when he designed La Tourette, and I felt that the metaphorical concepts would create a meaningful architecture for this project.

When I designed the Mission of St. Mary, I contemplated the Caravaggio painting *The Calling of Saint Matthew*, in which the light filters expressively over a wall. This led to a study of the chiaroscuro movement, which inspired me to create the altar painting. It's the coupling aspect of ideas like these that give our buildings a higher purpose. It may not be obvious—and it actually should never be obvious, but it's something that we as designers can reference. These ideas are metaphorical but in no way are they gratuitous.

After you've let ideas percolate, how do you know you're ready to begin the physical aspects of the design?

Robert McCarter and I asked Steven Holl to come to the University of Florida about fifteen years ago to give a lecture. Steve made a statement to me that had a significant impact on me as a practicing architect. He remarked that the hardest thing about creating good architecture today is discovering how to practice the discipline of resistance: how to deny the urge to come to a solution too quickly, how to resist rushing even though we're always fighting against time. Projects have schedules and budgets, so how can we give that fermentation period enough time is an ongoing

↑ THE LYRICAL AESTHETICS OF THE SCHOOL REFLECT THE FACT THAT ITS STUDENTS ARE MUSICALLY GIFTED, SHOWN IN THE PATTERNING ON THE UPPER MASSING AND IN THE LOWER YELLOW FORM THAT "FOLDS" INTO IT.

question. I think this is why we are never truly finished with our projects, why we are designing to the very end.

In his essay, Gwathmey speaks of paradox in your work—the rational and the romantic, the rigorous and the poetic. How does this paradoxical quality relate to your creative process?

I think the reason Kahn said that architecture is an old man's profession is because we're constantly trying to learn the craft of architecture coupled with the art of architecture. When I say the craft, I mean connections—how materials

↓ ALFONSO OFTEN CREATES PAINTINGS IN ORDER TO IDENTIFY THE "SOUL" OF A PROJECT. HERE, HE WAS REFERENCING THE RELIGIOUS BELIEFS OF THE CLIENTS FOR WHOM HE'S DESIGNING THE RESIDENCE.

PATEL 5 ELEMENTS

meet and how we can express ideas in a very clear, rational way. When a steel beam is meeting a wood panel, how do they meet? There has to be some point of transition. When you look at our work you'll see the Miesian concept of form-giving. In this respect, we try to make things very honest.

We couple that with the intuitive as it relates to say, Corb, who would set up a Miesian rational grid and then violate it with a cubist or an organic shape. This creates a tension that becomes paradoxical. The way Mies accomplished the same duality was to place a Calder sculpture in front of a building. The two are like a marriage that works, and the duality of opposites brings richness to a building.

You often speak of self-awareness and authenticity. How can you explain these concepts as they relate to your architecture?

I have been working on a lecture called "The Rational and the Intuitive" for several years. Each time I give it, the ideas expressed in it evolve because I challenge each person in the audience to contemplate his or her personal core, and the discussions are always lively and informative. I encourage each person in the room to ask, What is the well that you can draw from that makes your work different? What influences, whether music or art or food or family, can you reference?

Every architect or artist studies other work, but it's our duty as creative human beings to reinterpret rather than to simply copy. I'm reminded of how the Beatles, after listening to Roy Orbison, took one of his melodies, sped it up, put words to it, and created "Please Please Me." Were they copying him? No, they were taking what he had created and putting it through their own artistic filter.

I think it's important for students to learn how to extract the essence of self from life and to ask how this informs their work. I have many influences that continually inform my work. In film, it may be Fellini and Bergman; in music, the Beatles and Stan Getz are unswerving inspirations.

Do you sketch?

I sketch throughout the entire process. I am grounded in an old-school Bauhaus methodology that upholds drawings and physical models as critical. Although the computer is an incredible tool, the problem with it is that it can fool you into thinking you've arrived too soon because whatever you are designing looks so complete. It can trick you into misunderstanding spatially what you've drawn. We like to build a variety of rough, three-dimensional study models to help us understand what we're doing spatially before we turn to computer-generated drawings.

It's troubling to me that young architects are graduating from architecture school without drawing skills. I was talking to a professor at the University of Florida not long ago, and he commented that he has seen a backlash regarding computer-driven curriculum because his students are now saying they want to learn to draw. I think tradition is coming full circle in that regard. There's something romantic and tactile about holding a pencil to make a sketch.

When I sit on juries and critique students' projects at the university, I will invariably ask them where their sketches are. Often there are none, and that's unacceptable to me. Think about the sketches of da Vinci, for example, or about how Corb always had a sketchbook with him. I don't even believe that someone has to draw well to investigate spa-

↑ AN EARLY SKETCH FOR VENU, A MIXED-USE DEVELOPMENT IN DOWNTOWN TAMPA, IS AN EXAMPLE OF HOW EXPRESSIVE SIMPLY DRAWN LINES CAN BE.

tial ideas. If you look at Corb's early sketches, say during the time he took the tour of the Orient, they were almost photoreal. Then he developed this ability to minimize the lines. I love Picasso's statement that he spent the first half of his life learning to draw and the second half learning to draw like a child in order to capture the essence of something in just a few lines.

Is finding the soul of a project, as you call it, usually an easy process?

If I haven't found that unmeasurable aspect of the project early, I'm in trouble. The coupling of a big idea to guide the process while solving the pragmatics always gives us a reference to return to. Discovering the essence that launches us and serves as a guiding compass throughout the project is never easy but is always fulfilling.

Do you travel for inspiration?

There's a particular town in Italy, which the Etruscans founded, that I visit as often as possible. Because it cascades down the side of a mountain, there's only one level street and not a single straight street within its perimeter. This produces a constant, three-dimensional layering of mass and void that is always in movement. When I experience the shifting perspective of these streets that wind up and in and around, it helps me to understand that space is never static; that space should always be perceived in relation to movement and position.

When I'm there, I also notice a dichotomy between the American culture and the Italian culture that affects me. The Italians work to live and we Americans live to work. Life there is permeated with real freedom, and I decompress immediately. In that decompression, I'm able to reconnect with myself, to stand at a distance and look back. This gives me the opportunity to see my work historically and with clarity.

← A GRACEFUL OCULAR WINDOW ON THE NIELSEN MEDIA RESEARCH CAMPUS FRAMES A BRONZE SCULPTURE, ILLUSTRATING THE EXPRESSIVE-NESS OF ALFONSO'S COUPLING OF THE RATIONAL AND THE POETIC.

You were born to Cuban parents—do you feel that a Latin romanticism influences your work?

I paint and my father painted. I think our Latin sensibilities mean that we gravitate toward organic things—color and shapes, which come out in our work. Also, there's something about being Cuban that is innately expressive and optimistic, even sarcastic. Cubans are known to laugh at themselves. I guess it comes down to an enjoyment of life that overflows into my work.

We enjoy what we do here at the firm, and I would say that to some extent this is an extension of the Cuban heritage that I share with my brother, Carlos, who has also been a driving force behind the firm and in my life. We have been able to develop a practice in which we can be expressive and passionate about our work.

When you were a child, were there signs that you would be involved in architecture?

I don't remember a time when I didn't know that I was going to be an architect. I think this stems from the incredible admiration I had for my father. I saw that architecture was such a cool profession and he was a heroic figure in my life.

How does working in Florida inform your work?

The incredible light that we have here, the harsh climate that we have to deal with, and the specifics of siting buildings in the tropics are common denominators in every project we undertake. For example, the intense light provides wonderful opportunities for investigations, not only in reference to light and shadow but also in reference to the movement of the light. We must ask, Is the light focused or flooded? Is it direct from the south or indirect from the north? What happens spatially as it rotates around the project? In answering these questions and others that relate to a project's environment, elements such as the light, the rain, the breezes, and the heat become tools for us to support our strategies, whether they are measurable or unmeasureable.

Have you seen a progression in your work since your early days as an architect?

Yes, of course. For example, there is a dichotomy in our current work that stems from more intensive editing combined with greater risk-taking. Our projects are bigger and the civic responsibility is greater, so the expectations are higher. The pressure can also be greater because we never want to miss opportunities to be more expressive and to create significant architecture.

I am currently designing two museums for which we are pushing considerably on the sculptural quality of the public spaces while resisting the urge to overdesign the galleries. Early in my career, my father gave me the opportunity to design, which helped me to get some things out of my system. In my first house, I used every curve I could imagine! My work is more mature now, and it has a conscious bent toward creating timeless architecture. I just turned fifty and I've been at this for over twenty-five years. That naturally brings a fair amount of perspective.

UNIVERSITY OF SOUTH FLORIDA PSYCHOLOGY/COMMUNICATION DISORDERS BUILDING, 2001

Tampa, Florida

Situated between the fine arts and medical districts, and bounded on the north by predefined pedestrian and vehicular corridors, the parti of this inaugural building in a new campus district developed as a figurative and literal bridge. Its design evolved as an east/west linear bar stretching along the pedestrian corridor with a programmatic split over the existing road and utility easement. The Florida AIA honored Alfonso Architects with a Merit Award for the design of this 110,000-square-foot building.

↓ THE BAR OF THE FIVE-HUNDRED-FOOT-LONG FACADE PEELS AWAY, CREATING A SUBTLE BUT HIGHLY EXPRESSIVE ARC.

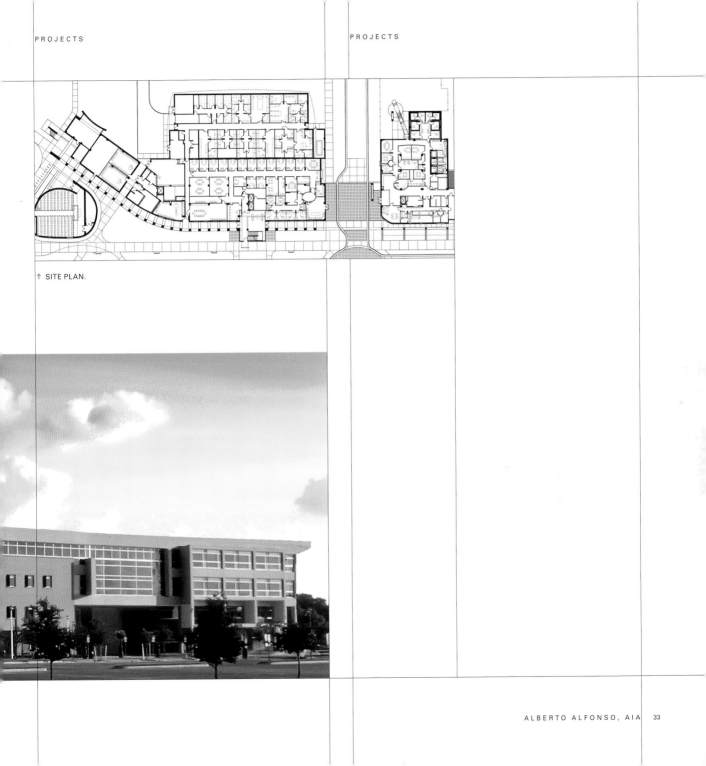

↑ SITE PLAN.

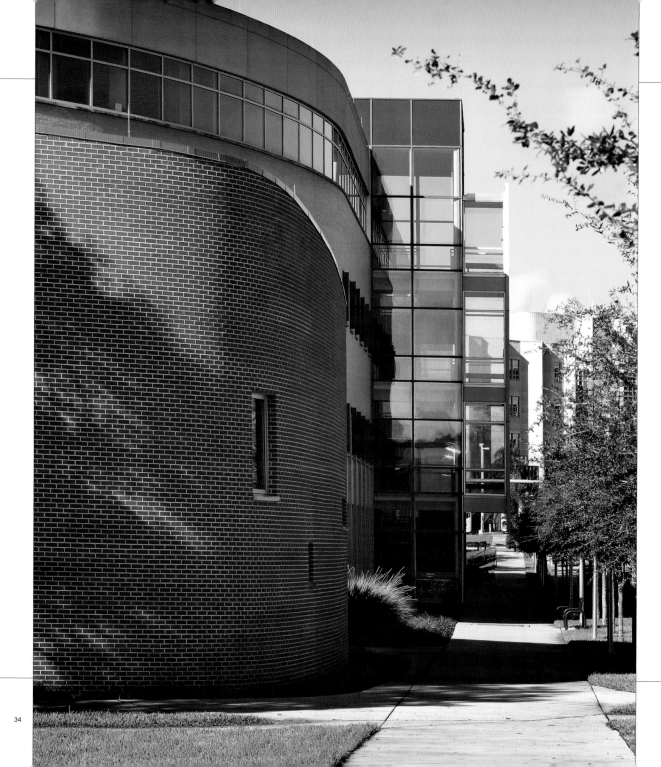

↑ THE MOVEMENT OF THE SUSPENDED STAIRWELL IS DRAMATIC IN ITS GLASS VOLUMETRIC.

← ALFONSO'S RECURRING THEME OF MIXING SOLID AND TRANSPARENT FORMS SHOWS ITSELF HERE IN THE COMBINATION OF A CURVED BRICK MASS AND A TRANSPARENT GLASS BOX.

↓ ELEVATIONS.

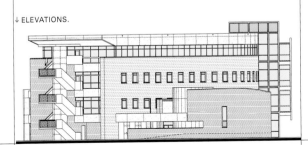

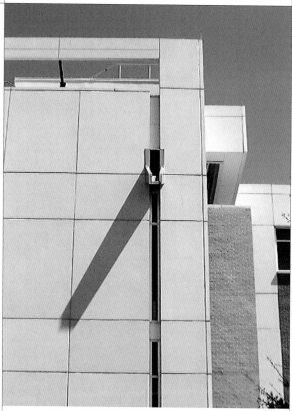

↑ THE MIX OF MATERIALS ON THE FACADE CREATES TEXTURAL INTEREST.

↑ MULLION FINS SERVE AS SUN PROTECTION, AND SHADOW-BOX WINDOWS ARE CONTRASTING ELEMENTS IN SHAPE AND TONALITY.

↑ THE ARC OF THE BUILDING FORMS A DYNAMIC ELEMENT IN THE PRECAST CONCRETE ROOFLINE.

← A FLUTED WALL OF SCORED CONCRETE REINFORCES THE ROOF DETAIL.

↑ THE BUILDING SPLAYS TOWARD THE SOUTH ON EACH END. A RIBBON
OF WINDOWS ABUTTING THE ROOFLINE CREATES THE ILLUSION THAT THE
ROOF FLOATS ABOVE THE FACADE.

NIELSEN MEDIA RESEARCH, 2003

Oldsmar, Florida

Completed in two phases, this 600,000-square-foot project for the international media consultant took its cues from the rhythmic patterning of the computer punch card. To imply the "idea" of data, the design included rigorously planned random fenestrations and a glazing system that varied the color and opacity of the glass. Alfonso Architects was awarded an Unbuilt Award for the design of this project, and each phase garnered the firm an Award of Excellence in design from the Florida Association of the American Institute of Architects (AIA). The firm also won an Honor Award for Architecture from the Tampa Bay AIA for the project.

→ GLASS IN FOUR VARYING HUES, EACH PANEL FRAMED WITH INTRICATE MULLION FINS THAT SHIELD THE INTERIORS FROM THE STRONG FLORIDA SUNLIGHT, CREATES PATTERNING ON THE EXTERIOR OF THE BUILDING. THE DINING HALL IS A MIESIAN-INSPIRED GLASS PAVILION.

PAGES 42–43
→ BECAUSE AN IMPERATIVE FOR THE DESIGN OF THIS PROJECT WAS CONTROLLING THE INTENSE NATURAL LIGHT THAT TRAVERSES THE CAMPUS EACH DAY, LOUVERS WERE PLACED EVERY FOUR FEET, FORMING A BRISE-SOLEIL TO OFFER SHADING.

→→ THIS CLOSE-UP OF THE METAL MULLION FINS ON THE SOUTH-FACING FACADE SHOWS ALFONSO'S RIGOROUS ATTENTION TO DETAILING.

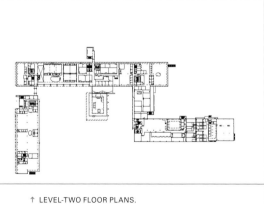

↑ LEVEL-TWO FLOOR PLANS.

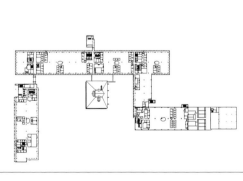

↑ LEVEL-THREE FLOOR PLANS.

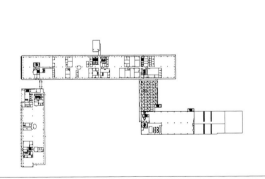

↑ LEVEL-FOUR FLOOR PLANS.

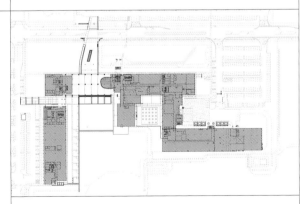

↑ SITE PLAN.

↑ ALFONSO COMMISSIONED BERNIE VOICHYSONK, WHO HAD STUDIED
UNDER THE GERMAN PAINTER AND EDUCATOR JOSEF ALBERS, TO PAINT A
MURAL THAT WOULD REFLECT THE SUN'S MOVEMENT ACROSS THE CAMPUS.

↑ THIS VIEW OF THE CAFETERIA ILLUSTRATES HOW THE FREE PLAN
STRIKINGLY OPENS A SPACE TO THE OUTDOORS. THE PATTERNING IN THE
CARPETING WAS DESIGNED AS A NOD TO THE COMPANY'S PURPOSE,
THE COLLECTION OF DATA.

↑ WINDOWS THAT WERE PUSHED INTO THE SOUTH-FACING FACADE OF
THE DATA CENTER CREATE A BRISE-SOLEIL WITH A SHADOW-BOX EFFECT.

PROJECTS

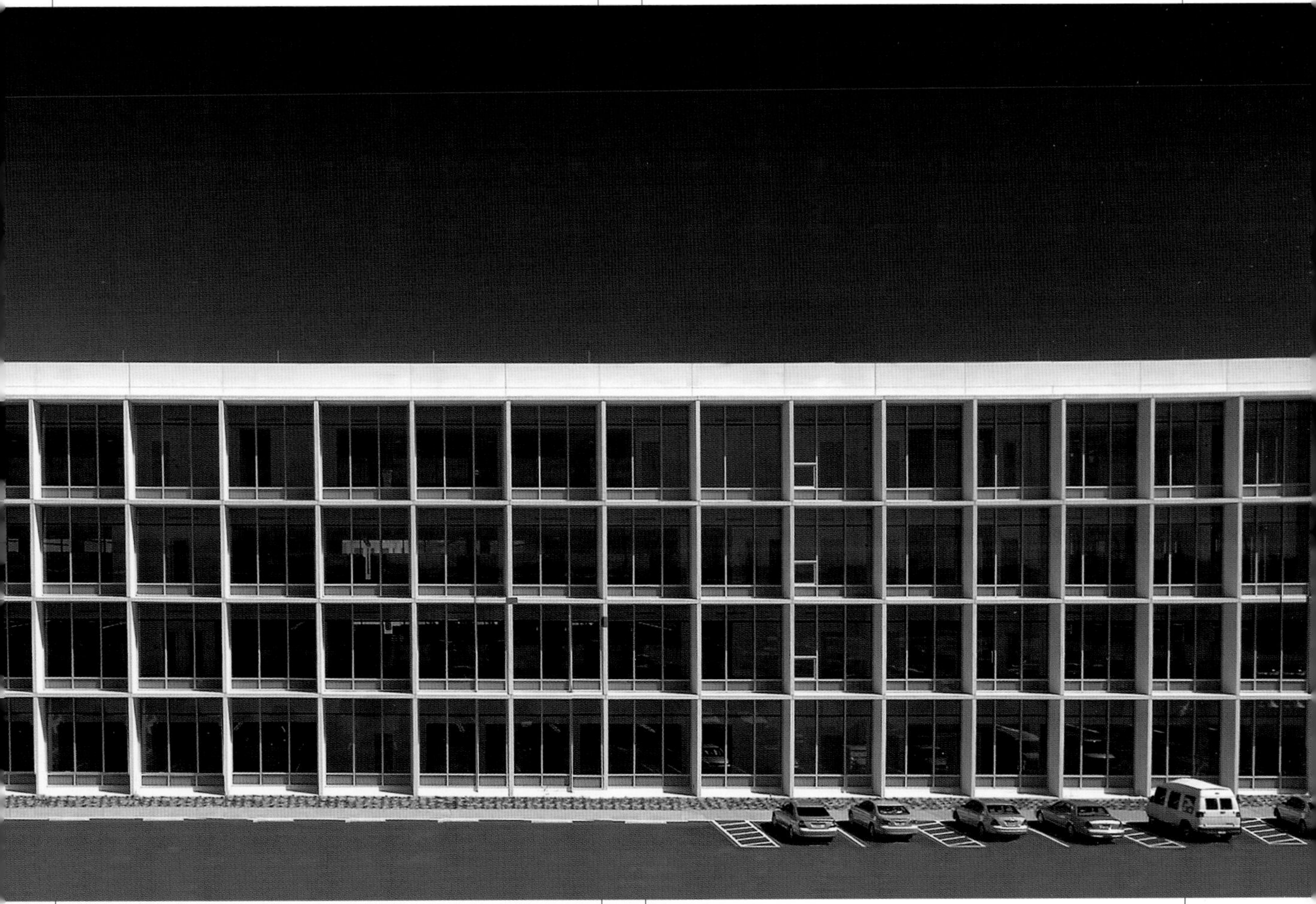

AIRSIDE C, TAMPA INTERNATIONAL AIRPORT, 2004

Tampa, Florida

Alfonso's mission for the 315,000-square-foot, sixteen-gate terminal was to express the drama and excitement of travel through architecture. By warping and weaving the geometries of the oval and the wing, the firm synthesized a new shape, the "woval," which created a freeform roof plane. Through a blending of forms and movements, the airside becomes a static pause in space and time that allows travelers to realize the importance of place before they move on to their destinations. The design of this project won Alfonso Architects a Florida AIA Award of Excellence in 2007 and a Merit Award from the Tampa Bay AIA.

→ THE WEIGHTLESSNESS OF THE ROOF PLANE EMPHASIZES LIGHTNESS AND FLIGHT. GWATHMEY DESCRIBES THE BUILDING AS ASYMMETRICAL, ORGANIC, SPATIALLY SENSUOUS, VOLUMETRICALLY DYNAMIC, AND MATERIALLY DENSE.

↑ FINAL BOARDING CALL, A PAINTING BY CHRISTOPHER STILL (2005), SET THE TONE FOR THE AIRSIDE C PROJECT AT THE TAMPA INTERNATIONAL AIRPORT.

← CURVILINEAR WALLS OF BRAZILIAN WALNUT AND PANELS OF SAND-BLASTED GLASS ARE LIGHT/DARK, MASSIVE/ETHEREAL ELEMENTS IN THE AREA APPROACHING THE GATES. EAMES SHELL ROCKERS RECALL THE JET-SET ERA.

→ MOSAICS IN THE FLOOR CORRELATE WITH FIBERGLASS TUBES THAT PROTRUDE FROM THE CEILING AND SERVE AS LIGHT WELLS IN THE TRAM ENTRY/EXIT FOYER.

↑ THE CARPET PATTERN IN THE GATE AREA WAS DESIGNED TO EVOKE
FLYING INTO AND OUT OF TAMPA, WHEN TRAVELERS PASS OVER
A PATCHWORK OF FLORIDA LAKES. THE SEATING IS CLASSIC EAMES.

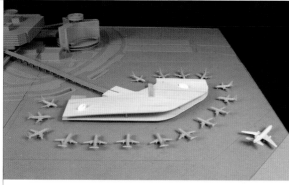

↑ THE MODEL OF AIRSIDE C SHOWS HOW THE ROOF IS PINCHED ON EITHER END, LEAVING THE WEIGHTIER MIDDLE SECTION TO MARK THE PORTION OF THE TERMINAL THAT HOLDS THE HIGHEST DENSITY OF PEOPLE.

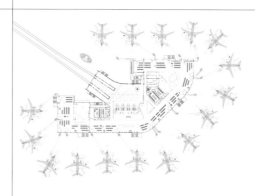

↑ FLOOR PLAN FOR AIRSIDE C.
↓ TO ACHIEVE THE TEXTURALLY RICH FINISH ON THE CONCRETE, ALFONSO HAD THE SURFACE IMPRINTED WITH STRIPS OF WOOD.

MISSION OF ST. MARY, 2005

Tampa, Florida

Situated in a transient, low-income, suburban neighborhood, the Mission of St. Mary is a 4,000-square-foot open-air pavilion that was devised to provide shelter, direction, and opportunities for the expression of faith to members of the surrounding community. Demands of the project were that the building, which is comprised of metal and stucco-on-block elements floating beneath a preengineered metal roof structure, be durable and meet a very limited budget. A reduced-height screen-wall that extends to the south acts as the processional wall for the fourteen stations of the Way of the Cross. The design of this project won Alfonso Architects Unbuilt and Honor Awards from the Florida AIA, and the H. Dean Rowe Award of Design Excellence from the Tampa Bay AIA.

→ THE MODEL OF THE MISSION OF ST. MARY ILLUSTRATES HOW ITS ROOF PLANE FLOATS ABOVE THE CURVED WALL OF THE CHAPEL, ITS RIBS PROVIDING STRUCTURE AND DRAMA.

→ THE CANTILEVERED ROOF IS A DOMINANT ELEMENT IN THE DESIGN, OFFERING SHELTER WHILE LEAVING COMMUNICANTS OPEN TO NATURE.

→→ THE PEWS AND THE ALTAR CAN BE REARRANGED TO ACCOMMODATE ATTENDANCE LEVELS FROM INTIMATE GATHERINGS TO HOLY-DAY CROWDS, MAKING THE SANCTUARY, WITH ITS GRACEFULLY ARCING WALL, AN AGILE BUILDING.

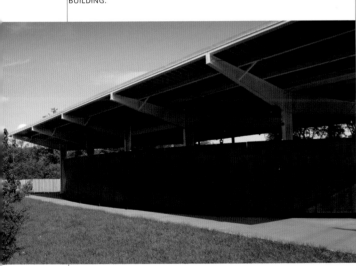

↑ THE OPEN-AIR PAVILION, COMPRISED OF STUCCO AND PREENGINEERED METAL, HAS A CURVED SANCTUARY WALL THAT LEVITATES EIGHT INCHES ABOVE GRADE.

↑ THE ENTRY TO THE CHAPEL IS A PROGRESSION FROM BRIGHT NATURAL LIGHT TO SHADED INTERIOR, THE PROTECTION FROM SUNLIGHT ACHIEVED WITH AMPLE CANTILEVERED OVERHANGS.

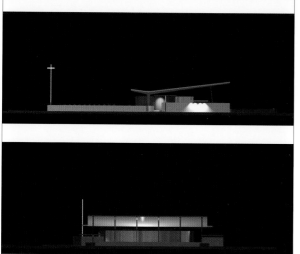

↑ ELEVATIONS OF THE BUILDING SHOW HOW THE ROOF ARCS HEAVENWARD.

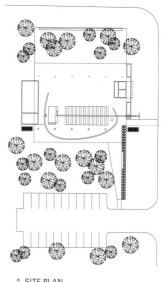

↑ SITE PLAN.

↑ ALFONSO'S DESIGNS FOR THE STATIONS OF THE CROSS.

↑ STATIONS OF THE CROSS HAVE BEEN SCULPTED FROM METAL PLACARDS
ON A REDUCED-HEIGHT SCREEN-WALL THAT EXTENDS FROM THE CHAPEL.
WHEN SUNLIGHT BEAMS THROUGH THE IMAGES, IT REFLECTS THEM IN
A GHOSTLY SUBTLETY AGAINST THE WHITE WALL.

PROJECTS

SAM RAMPELLO DOWNTOWN PARTNERSHIP SCHOOL, 2005

Tampa, Florida

The urban site for this 110,000-square-foot K–8 school is surrounded by heavy vehicular traffic on all sides except the southern face, where the pace is slowed by pedestrian traffic. The buildings were pushed to the edges of the site, creating an interior courtyard where the children could gather. The main entry was placed on the passive southern edge. For the design process, Alfonso collaborated with a composer to create a musical piece, the progression of which parallels the expression of the architecture. The State of Florida AIA awarded Alfonso Architects Unbuilt and Merit Awards for this project.

→ PATTERNS FOR THE RIGOROUSLY PLANNED RANDOM FENESTRATIONS AND COLORED PANELS WERE DEVELOPED AS AN ABSTRACTION OF THE MUSICAL PIECE CREATED FOR THE DESIGN OF THE SCHOOL.

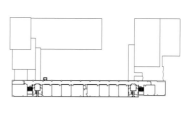

↑ LEVEL-THREE FLOOR PLAN.

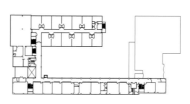

↑ LEVEL-TWO FLOOR PLAN.

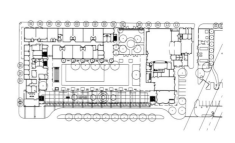

↑ LEVEL-ONE FLOOR PLAN.

↑↑ THE MIDDLE SCHOOL BUILDING APPEARS TO HOVER WITHIN ITS URBAN SETTING, AND THE HOLLOWED-OUT BELLY CREATES A COVERED WALKWAY.

↑ CONTRASTING WITH THE PALE, FLOATING FORM OF THE MIDDLE SCHOOL BUILDING IS THE GROUNDED, COLORFUL FORM OF THE ELEMENTARY SCHOOL WITH ITS BREEZEWAYS THAT OPEN ONTO THE CENTRAL COURTYARD.

↑↑ THE VOLUMES AND MASSES OF THE BUILDINGS REPRESENT LAYERS OF MEANING, FROM THE SWELL OF A MASSIVE RECTANGLE TO THE ANCHOR OF A SMALLER CONNECTING RECTANGULAR SHAPE—A GRAPHIC LANGUAGE THAT IS NOT UNLIKE THE RISE AND FALL OF A MUSICAL CADENCE.

↑ THE PLAYGROUND IS SET WITHIN A PERIMETER OF BUILDINGS; THEIR ARRANGEMENT WAS DESIGNED TO ACT AS A SHELTER FROM THE HARSHNESS OF THE URBAN SETTING.

↑↑ IN THIS VIEW OF THE COURTYARD, THE OPEN BREEZEWAY UNDER THE MIDDLE SCHOOL BUILDING IS VISIBLE. RAISED COLUMNS ON THE FACADE HEIGHTEN THE GEOMETRIC COMPLEXITY OF HORIZONTAL AND VERTICAL FORMS.

↑ MODERN INFLUENCES MAKE THE BUILDING'S INTERLOCKING LINES, PATTERNS, AND FORMS DYNAMICALLY RICH. THE FACADE CONNOTES A MUSICAL SCORE THANKS TO ALFONSO'S CAREFUL PLANNING.

LAKE HOUSE #1, 2006

Tampa, Florida

Situated on a lakefront site in central Florida, this 6,200-square-foot residence was designed as a family-friendly home that maintains a clear separation between the spaces within which the adults' and the children's activities take place. Because of the copse of mature oak trees into which the home is nestled, a horizontal transparency was possible for the north, south, and east facades. A floating "sun ribbon" at the second floor wraps the three facades to create a unifying element.

→ THE DESIGN STRATEGY FOR THIS RESIDENCE WAS AN ELONGATED PARTI THAT STEPS DOWN TOWARD AND CULMINATES AT THE LAKE.

↑↑ THE MASSING OF THE HOUSE MOVES FROM VERY DENSE, A TRAVERTINE BOX, TO VERY LIGHT, A GLASS PAVILION THAT IS NESTLED INTO A POCKET OF TREES.

↑ A CONICAL DRUM THAT FRAMES AN INTERIOR STAIRWELL PROTRUDES FROM THE GLASS BOX, WHICH HOLDS THE MAIN LIVING ROOM.

→ LOOKING FROM THE HOUSE TOWARD THE LAKE, THE SLOPE OF THE ROOF ON THE POOL HOUSE DIRECTS THE EYE TOWARD THE WATER, ILLUSTRATING HOW THE COMPOSITIONAL COLLAGE REACHES A REFINED LEVEL OF RESOLUTION.

↑ THE STAIRWAY THAT RISES ABOVE THE MAIN ENTRY SEEMS TO FLOAT AS IT CLIMBS TOWARD THE GLASS BOX PROTRUDING ABOVE THE ENTRY PROMONTORY.

↑ THE CURVING PLASTER STAIR IS A COMMANDING ELEMENT IN THE LIVING ROOM PAVILION.

→ BECAUSE THE LIVING ROOM PAVILION IS SO TRANSPARENT, ALFONSO DESIGNED AN EXPOSED RIB CEILING TO GROUND AND ENRICH THE SPACE.

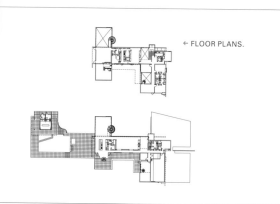

← FLOOR PLANS.

UNIVERSITY OF SOUTH FLORIDA CHILDREN'S MEDICAL SERVICES AND SCHOOL OF NURSING, 2006

Tampa, Florida

These two buildings form a campus gateway and an updated image for the section of the university campus where they are located. The 100,000-square-foot educational facility is a three-story addition to and renovation of an existing nursing education building, which provides new teaching and testing environments. The interior and exterior of the 60,000-square-foot medical office building reference playful gestures in keeping with the clinic's mission to serve children while also providing administrative space for campus and state healthcare entities.

→ THE CURTAIN WALL OF THE CHILDREN'S MEDICAL SERVICES BUILDING IS PUSHED BACK INTO AN ABSTRACT BOX FORMED BY A FLOATING ROOF OVERHANG AND WALL PROTRUSIONS. THE OVERHANG IS ECHOED BY A PLINTH, WHICH WILL SERVE AS A BASE FOR A SCULPTURE.

↓ SITE PLAN FOR THE UNIVERSITY OF SOUTH FLORIDA MEDICAL CAMPUS, WHICH INCLUDES A NUMBER OF BUILDINGS DESIGNED BY ALFONSO ARCHITECTS.

PROJECTS

↑ THE SOLID MASSING, WITH ITS SCORED PLASTER, COLORFUL GLASS, AND ABSTRACT WINDOW PATTERNS, PROVIDES AN OPAQUE ELEMENT TO CONTRAST WITH THE BUILDING'S MASSIVE TRANSPARENT CURTAIN WALL. A PORTION OF THE WALL IS WRAPPED WITH A SOLID OVERLAY THAT SEEMS TO FLOAT AS IT FOLDS DOWNWARD.

→ THE ENTRY DRUM WRAPS INTO THE INTERIOR OF THE BUILDING, CREATING A COMMANDING SCULPTURAL ELEMENT AND DELINEATING AN INTIMATELY SCALED "ROOM" WITHIN THE EXPANSIVE LOBBY AREA.

↑ THIRD-FLOOR PLAN.

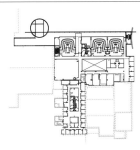

↑ SECOND-FLOOR PLAN.

↑ INSIDE THE BUILDING, ALFONSO CARVED RECTANGULAR PUNCTURES FROM THE WALLS IN ABSTRACT PATTERNS, ECHOING THE FENESTRATIONS ON THE EXTERIOR.

↓ THIS STUDY OF THE FACADE OF THE SCHOOL OF NURSING BUILDING ILLUSTRATES ALFONSO'S DESIRE TO CREATE A CONICAL DRUM TO HOLD THE STAIRWELL, WHICH HE WOULD CLAD IN ALUMINUM PANELS.

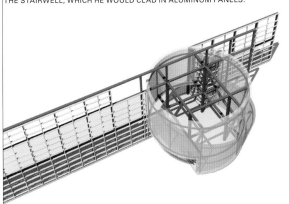

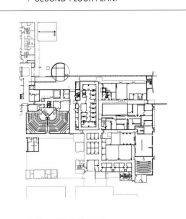

↑ FIRST-FLOOR PLAN.

↑ A FREEFORM FRAME TIES THE SKELETAL GRID OF THE BUILDING TO THE ENTRY DRUM AND OTHER DISPARATE ELEMENTS.

↑ A PORTION OF THE CYLINDRICAL ELEMENT HAS BEEN CARVED AWAY IN ORDER TO OPEN IT TO VIEWS OF WATER, WHICH REPRESENTS HEALING.

↑ THE SCHOOL OF NURSING BUILDING WAS THE FIRST THAT ALFONSO
ARCHITECTS DESIGNED FOR THE UNIVERSITY. THE NORTH-FACING CURTAIN
WALL IS ANCHORED ON THE END BY THE ENTRY DRUM.

FLAGLER CONSTRUCTION, 2007

Fort Myers, Florida

The challenge with this project was to develop a prototype building using the strategy of a "kit-of-parts" that could be interchanged and implemented on any given site without costly customization. Materials and structural systems were chosen from off-the-shelf items and were detailed in an atypical way to achieve a unique aesthetic.

↓ A BRISE-SOLEIL SCREEN FRAMES THE SERVICE BAY. THE INNER ROOFLINE EXTENDS UP AND BEYOND THE OUTER MASSING, CREATING A FORM WITHIN A FORM.

→ THE SEMI-TRANSPARENT SCREEN OF THE BRISE-SOLEIL CREATES AN OUTDOOR ROOM.

↓ THE INTERIORS ARE MACHINE-ART SIMPLE, WITH POWERFUL MATERIAL DETAILING.

VENU, 2007 (unbuilt)

Tampa, Florida

VENU, a mixed-use development in downtown Tampa, is comprised of a twin-formed, fifty-story tower—a portion of which is solid while the other is sculpturally transparent. Located on the Hillsborough River at the intersection of Kennedy Boulevard and Ashley Drive, the site represents the downtown axis, or the "living room," of the city. The riverside project provides a link in the Tampa Riverwalk project that connects to the cultural arts district.

↓ INTENDED AS A DIALOGUE BETWEEN TWO RECTANGLES, ONE MASS AND ONE TRANSPARENT, THE COMPOSITION ACCENTUATES THE HEIGHT AND SLENDERNESS OF THE BUILDING.

↑↑ AS A CULTURAL DESTINATION, VENU'S RELATIONSHIP TO ITS URBAN CONTEXT IS ENRICHED BY ITS STREET-LEVEL ATTRIBUTES—A MUSEUM AND A CAFÉ.

↑ VENU'S TWIN SKINS ARE GLASS AND PERFORATED METAL PANELS. A CANTILEVERED CANOPY ANNOUNCES THE CAFÉ ENTRANCE ON THE GLASS FACADE, WHILE THE PANELED FACADE FLOATS ABOVE THE ATTENDANT PLAZA.

← THE SPIRE OF THE GLASS TOWER RISES SKYWARD ABOVE THE HILLSBOROUGH RIVER.

LAKE HOUSE #2, 2007

Tampa, Florida

This 24,000-square-foot residence in central Florida was designed for a twenty-acre parcel of lakefront property. The Hindu beliefs of the husband and wife drove the parti of this project into deep symbolic histories and meanings, resulting in a "great hall" that symbolizes the paternal and a "performance hall" that reflects the maternal love for music and botanicals.

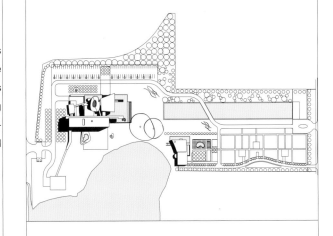

→ SITE PLAN.

↓ THE MODEL, WHICH IS A STUDY IN VITALITY, SHOWS THAT THE RESIDENCE WILL BE PLACED ON A PLINTH OF WATER, SYMBOLIC OF ITS OBJECTIFIED DETACHMENT FROM THE LITERAL.

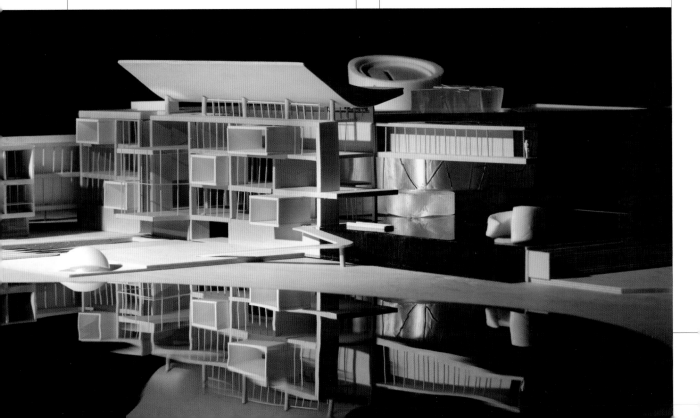

↓ SKETCHED AND PAINTED STUDIES OF LAKE HOUSE #2 EMPHASIZE
THE INTERPLAY OF SHADOW AND LIGHT—AN OVERARCHING THEME
FOR THIS HOME.

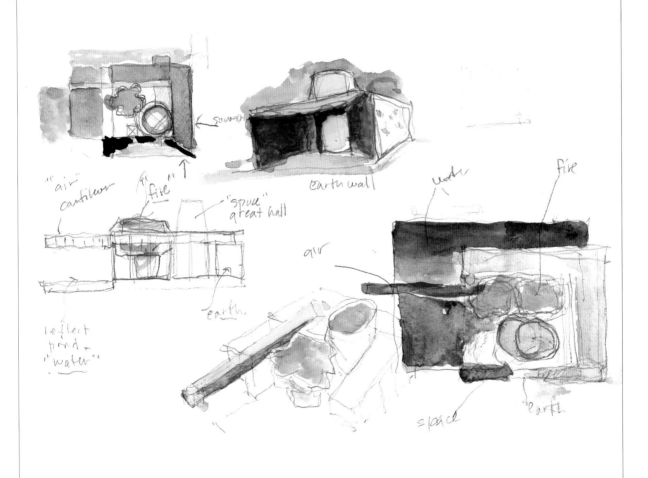

UNIVERSITY OF SOUTH FLORIDA CENTER FOR ADVANCED HEALTH-CARE NORTH, 2008

Tampa, Florida

This 215,000-square-foot project includes new facilities for clinical and patient care services, an ambulatory procedure center, and a clinical research facility. Situated in the burgeoning healthcare quadrant of the campus, the structure sits at the opposite end of a courtyard from the Medical Faculty Office Building.

→ THE BUILDING'S LINEAR QUALITY IS HEIGHTENED BY ITS WINDOW FENESTRATIONS, BROKEN ONLY BY A GLASS BOX RAISED ON PILOTIS ABOVE THE ENTRY.

← THE RELATIONSHIP OF THE HORIZONTAL AND VERTICAL ELEMENTS ON THE FACADE CREATES TENSION. THE CURTAIN WALL IS BEAUTIFULLY TRANSPARENT, WHILE THE GLASS PLANK RECTANGLE IS DRAMATICALLY OPAQUE.

↓ THE FACILITY WITH WHICH ALFONSO SEAMLESSLY MERGES HORIZONTAL AND VERTICAL ELEMENTS IS EVIDENT EVEN WHILE THE BUILDING IS UNDER CONSTRUCTION.

→ A MIX OF MATERIALS ON THE FACADE IS DEFTLY HANDLED, AND THE RIGOROUS PATTERNING OF HORIZONTAL AND VERTICAL ELEMENTS BRINGS THIS BUILDING THE ARCHITECTURAL RICHNESS THAT ALFONSO CHAMPIONS.

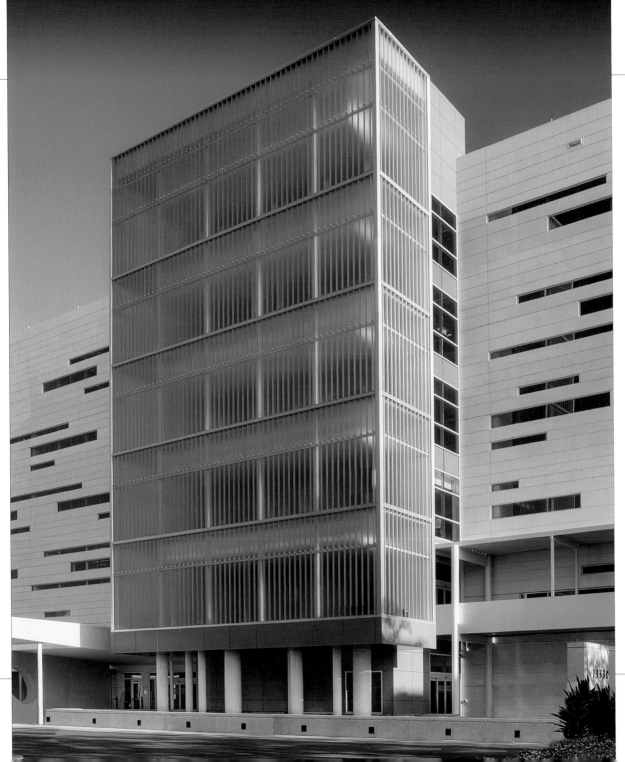

THE ARTS CENTER (in progress)

St. Petersburg, Florida

The Chihuly museum will be the centerpiece of the Arts Center's 133,000-square-foot contemporary art facility in downtown St. Petersburg. It will include a glassblowing hot-shop with auditorium seating, a nine-story studio/arts education tower, 27,000 square feet of galleries, and the 11,000-square-foot museum named for the celebrated glass artist.

↓ THE COMBINATION OF SOLID AND ETHEREAL MASSES IS A RECURRING THEME IN ALFONSO ARCHITECTS' BUILDINGS. THE ARTS CENTER IN ST. PETERSBURG IS NO EXCEPTION.

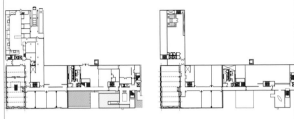

↑ FIRST-FLOOR PLAN

↑ SECOND-FLOOR PLAN

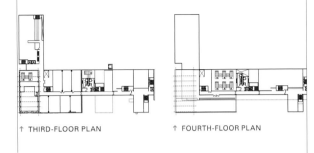

↑ THIRD-FLOOR PLAN

↑ FOURTH-FLOOR PLAN

↑ PAVILIONS PROTRUDE FROM THE MASSIVE CURTAIN WALL TOWARD THE STREET TO FRAME THE ENTRY WITH ITS CANTILEVERED OVERHANG. A COMBINATION OF TRANSPARENT AND OPAQUE FORMS ILLUSTRATES ALFONSO'S ABILITY TO CREATE SCULPTURALLY DYNAMIC ARCHITECTURE.

↑ INTERIORS OF THE ARTS CENTER ARE ARRANGED AROUND A CANTILEVERED STAIRWAY THAT FORMS ITS SPINE, LEAVING SPACES OPEN TO LIGHT AND VIEWS.

RENÉ GONZÁLEZ, AIA

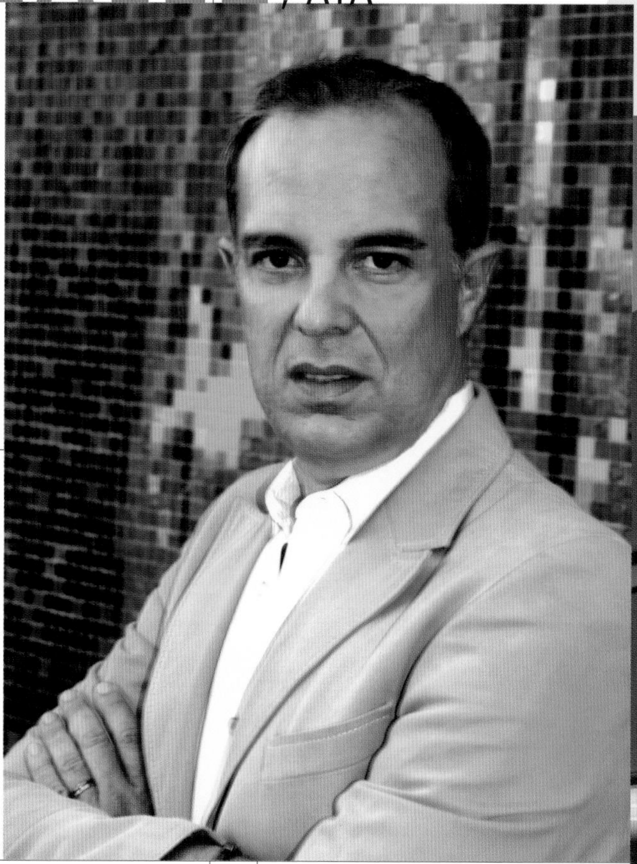

René González Architect | Miami, Florida

René González was born in Cuba. His family migrated to South Florida when he was three years old, and he grew up in the tropical surroundings that would come to have a significant influence on his design sensibilities.

González attended the University of Florida School of Architecture during his undergraduate years, studying under Martin Gundersen, for whom he served as a teaching assistant. "Martin's system of diagramming has stayed with me during my career," he says. "This rigor helped me tremendously in graduate school and it's something that I think about constantly when we're developing projects because these principles inform everything involved in organizing a program."

González left Florida to earn a Master of Architecture degree from UCLA. During his coursework, he attended studios led by Frank Israel and Richard Meier, and he would become a project designer for Meier on the Getty Center. He also collaborated with Israel during a time of extreme experimentation with materials and form, returning to Florida to oversee the construction of a residence on Jupiter Island that Israel had designed.

Once he returned to South Florida, González participated in another significant early collaboration, designing Wolfsonian Museum in Miami Beach with architect Mark Hampton, a member of the Sarasota School. As González

hit his stride in his career, he began teaching and lecturing at various universities, including UCLA, the University of Virginia, Florida International University, and a variety of institutions in South America.

In 1997, González opened his eponymous firm, creating a vehicle for the further exploration of materials and of the connection between the landscape and interiors. "Our approach is always holistic, meaning that we engage interiors and landscape, as well as architecture," he explains. "For each project, we research innovative materials, many from aeronautics and science."

Designing museums and gallery spaces has been a constant in González's career since the early days, and he continues to explore exhibition design for both public and private collections. His ability to create refined spaces for displaying art is the result of a rigorous distillation process. "How we think as architects is related to a process of questioning, a willingness to consistently ask about what we

→ THE ETHEREAL QUALITY OF THIS SPACE WITHIN KARLA ACCENTUATES RENÉ GONZÁLEZ'S PASSION FOR USING LIGHT AND MATERIALS TO CREATE THE EXPERIENTIAL.

↑ THE LAYERING OF SQUARE AND RECTANGULAR FORMS IN
GONZÁLEZ'S DESIGN OF THIS PALM BEACH HOUSE IS EVIDENT EVEN
IN THE SIMPLEST DETAILS.

see—filtering, distilling, adjusting focus on various aspects of the work," he remarks. "This process of inquiry leads to a quality of connection, whether it's with a site, a landscape, a client, a characteristic of light, an existing structure, or simply a concept. In turn, this connection is transformed into spatial realities."

The instinctual vocabulary that González employs to create architecture, which is at once powerful and serene, is likely the result of a collision of influences: the intuitive way of designing he was exposed to during his years in Los Angeles and the trajectory of modernism that flows through the sensibilities of his mentors, Meier among them.

ANALYSIS **by Richard Meier, FAIA, Principal of Richard Meier & Partners Architects, LLP, in New York and Los Angeles, Pritzker Prize winner**

Modern architecture is a progression. It is an ongoing dialogue between what was and what can be, and I am glad to see young architects like René González forging ahead with a vitality and discipline that keeps the continuum moving forward. As a modernist in South Florida, González faces a unique set of opportunities and challenges. Within Miami and its neighboring areas, the atmosphere seems charged with the connection between the old and the new, between the urban and the bucolic.

The tropical culture and climate offer a fertile context for expression, yet these same natural elements present a series of constraints for the architect. Melding the history and culture of South Florida and the principles of tropical design with the manipulation of light, geometry, and landscape as practiced in modernism requires a delicate act of balance. René González, refreshingly, seizes on the challenge articulated by Paul Ricoeur when he wrote that in pursuit of modernization we must "take root . . . in order to ceaselessly invent."[1]

Perhaps his early association with my friend, the Los Angeles architect Frank Israel, informed González's sensitivity to light, materials, and the individual nature of each site. Critical to the strong sense of space evinced by his work is the formation of light. The wood lattice system in his design for the Miami Museum of Contemporary Art lobby filters the light from the outside, casting a layer of illumination on the interior and framing the space in harmony with the entry plaza and courtyard. Beyond that, the materials and palette establish this point of entry as a portal to a museum of Miami and for Miami.

↓ THE WOOD LOUVERS IN THIS INDIAN CREEK HOME FILTER THE SUN'S RAYS, CREATING PATTERNS WITHIN ITS INDOOR AND OUTDOOR SPACES.

Similarly, González implements translucent panels to identify the space in his design for KARLA, a floral and event-planning company, which is housed in a converted warehouse. The shadow and light composing the backdrop of the space and its contents make the movement through the building a sensory experience. This connection between the human experience and the building is stirring in González's residential work as well. Indian Creek incorporates a series of pavilions enclosed with wood louvers and glass that not only filter the sun's rays but also dictate the light's composition and the patterns created within. The wood louvers bind the living spaces with light and the spirit of the tropics, while stone walls and reflecting pools inside the house harness the light by day and encourage movement and circulation.

The González program for a retreat in the Florida Keys makes the most of the connection between land and sea, elevating the building from the water with pilotis and incorporating a freely designed facade, which energizes the tension

between opacity and transparency. These elements combine with enclosed walkways and ramps to create a confluence and celebration of land, air, and water.

The order of geometry in architecture is a captivating enterprise in South Florida in that the landscape holds such sway over the building. The invocation of primary geometric forms, "beautiful forms because they are clearly legible," as Le Corbusier phrased it, to shape the dialogue between program and site yields affecting compositions when set against the backdrop of lush, and occasionally volatile, South Florida.[2]

The linear theme of René González's redesign of and addition to Maurice Fatio's 1936 Streamline Moderne house on the Atlantic Ocean in Palm Beach is informed entirely by the properties of the site. The layering of square and rectangular forms on the sprawling two-acre parcel of land, even in the vegetation, satisfies the obligation to order while drawing the inhabitant toward the ocean and points east. González's reorganization of the existing plan explores the relationship between vertical and horizontal spaces, in both the layout and the use of materials in the wall panels, windows, and pillars, creating areas of compression that clearly define the space within its tropical context. The efficacy of this plan is carried out to lyrical effect in a compact guesthouse in the Sunshine Ranches, whose simple layout is framed by rectangular wooden forms in the rafters and windows.

The most salient component of Florida architecture to enrich the modernist approach is the relationship between indoor and outdoor spaces. The balance between the two is where the intimacy of the region is most lucidly expressed. Consistent in González's work are flexible thresholds, which designate both garden and building as spaces for living. Interior spaces connect with, and at times dissolve into, the verdant lawns, bamboo, weeping ficus, and palm trees that are the timeless features of the region. In cultural spaces such as the Cisneros Fontanals Art Foundation, the vegetation and landscape direct the architecture, and the manmade elements of concrete, metal, tile, and stone are embedded within the jungle context.

In González's residential work, garden and pool are often enveloped within the house's boundaries. Most notably, in the open interior plan of his Key Biscayne house, there is a meditative pool in the center. The covered terraces, breezeways, cascading garden stairs, and fountains of the Palm Beach house pay tribute to the ideal of the tropical paradise, as do the gardens and reflecting pools of Indian Creek, which flow to the dissolving walls of the interior spaces. Here, too, the roof garden and roof lawn restore the land covered by the building. Without nostalgia, González is able to connect with the essence of the South Florida landscape and to create a sense of place for our time.

The configuration of volumes brought together in radiant light; the use of raw materials and geometric principles to bring spirit, harmony, and order to a space within a unique setting: these were the challenges and opportunities we had in the design of the Getty Center in Los Angeles. Modern architecture is a sensory pursuit as well as an intellectual one, rooted in the land and history of the places we inhabit. Just as the photosensitive glass in the roof of his Key Biscayne house shifts the hue and the intensity of the light in accordance with the time of day, so too does the work of René González evolve in its natural pattern.

← THE DESIGN OF THE CISNEROS FONTANALS ART FOUNDATION IS COMPOSED OF MANIPULATED NATURAL PATTERNS THAT DEPICT A TROPICAL JUNGLE.

↓ A MEDITATIVE POOL IS ENVELOPED WITHIN THE BOUNDARY OF THE KEY BISCAYNE HOUSE.

A Conversation with René González

Saxon Henry: How does building in South Florida inform your work?

I was raised in South Florida, so I think my affection for and my understanding of South Florida has to do with being raised here and with having memories of place, of spaces, of gardens, and of experiences.

I also studied in Los Angeles, which offers similar opportunities for the development of strong relationships between the interior and the exterior. This is something that I'm particularly interested in, so much so that I examined the relationships between the outside and the inside during my thesis. As a result, I have constructed a practice in which we generally work on an architecture that includes the development of the landscape and the interiors in a holistic way.

How would you describe the differences and similarities between designing architecture in Miami and Los Angeles?

There are similarities: the two cities are organized around the automobile. They both have edges that contain the city—in Miami and other South Florida cities, it's the Atlantic Ocean and the Everglades; in Los Angeles, it's the Pacific Ocean and the mountain ranges. These are urbanistic similarities.

But I also think there are significant differences: the climate in Los Angeles is temperate, whereas it's much more extreme here in South Florida. For example, we deal with the occurrence of hurricanes, which encourages us to think in creative ways in order to realize projects that we wouldn't otherwise be able to build. Also, Miami is a fresher, younger city, so there are positive opportunities that do not exist in Los Angeles, which is a more mature, established city.

Meier remarked in his essay that modern architecture is a sensory pursuit as well as an intellectual one. How much of your creative process is sensory and how much of it resides in the intellect?

It really is a combination. I start developing a project by exploring an initial idea, which we carry through the entire project. This is what organizes or modulates the project throughout the design process. Often there are times when I just feel that something needs to be adjusted or added or explored in a way that is different from that which the rationale would guide me to do. This is the sensory part of the process. By that I mean I may be developing the design of an elevation in a very rational way that is consistent with the language for the project, for example, but I might go back in and shift things around based on what feels right. In this way, though the process is a combination of very rational ordering principles that tend to be linear, it is also infused with intuition.

Where intuition can be very important is in designing an architecture that is meant to be experiential. I'm very interested in architecture that is experiential on many different levels, so it's important that the spaces evoke a certain feeling—be it dramatic or calming, or be it dynamic or static. At a smaller scale, it's important that the architecture touches man and that man touches the architecture. I want to build projects that physically engage people in the sense that they are lured to touch the walls, to have very tactile experiences.

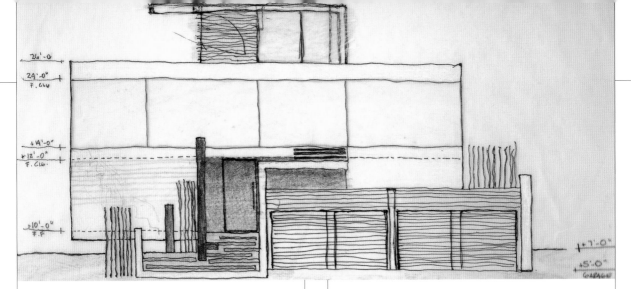

↑ AN EARLY SKETCH OF THE KEY BISCAYNE HOUSE.

How does your creative process show itself: swift lightning bolts or slow-to-reveal-themselves ideas?

For me, the creative process is passionate, enjoyable work. When I start a project, we do extensive research. We find a connection with the environment, with the site, with the client, with the program of the project, and then I start to look at the creative possibilities for the project. It's a process during which I'm always reexamining different possibilities, so it's a continuous exploration.

I also think that in order for architecture to be poetic, it has to have a soul, which means it has to have a strong idea behind it. In other words, the idea drives the project and the investigation or exploration that we undertake to create a project becomes the soul. When a project has this quality and is also rigorous in its architectural development, the two things combine to create a poetic experience. I think it's what anyone who strives to make architecture with a capital A works toward.

The process can be introspective at certain times, but it's not in any way mystical. It's real; it's about understanding something tangible. Sometimes that means that the creative process is about digging deep and finding the idea that's going to drive the thing, but sometimes it's about something as practical as the site, which is always extremely important to a project.

Meier notes that you connect with the South Florida landscape without nostalgia. Do you think this is true?

Yes, and I think that's very important for me. I've always believed that the buildings we build should be representative of our time and that they should not be nostalgic. The way that I enjoy developing projects is by understanding the place and by filtering the essence of those qualities that are found in that place. Then I believe it's important to reinterpret those qualities in ways that are developed without having any preconceived notions of what they should be in the final result.

It's beautiful to be able to make something that feels like it belongs in a place but that has no literal references. My goal is to create an implicit rather than an explicit architecture.

When you were growing up, were there signs that you would be involved in architecture?

I was always interested in architecture. I remember my brother and I would lay out relationships between urban environments as a game when we were young. By the time I was in high school, it was pretty clear that I wanted to study architecture, as I was already enrolled in an architecture program by then.

What has surprised you about being an architect?

I would have to say that it's the process of developing a practice, which has allowed me to understand the complexities of practicing. That's something that you can only learn once you have started to practice. It's something that is nearly impossible to get when you are in school. By that I mean the realities of building—how long a process it is; how you can be retained to develop a project and for one reason or another it isn't built; how many projects are actually built that you don't expect will go forward. It's a business and it's a profession, and at the same time it's a creative endeavor so it's a delicate balance. To maintain a design-intensive office requires a very delicate balance.

← EVEN WHEN THEY ARE TUCKED INTO URBAN SETTINGS, GONZÁLEZ'S EXTERIOR SPACES ACT AS OUTDOOR ROOMS.

I've also grown to understand what important collaborators our clients are. I always see the dialogue with our clients as extremely critical and I engage my clients in our work, always finding situations that we come across during the process of development as opportunities to rethink things.

Meier noted that you have a flair for a manipulation of light. How important is light when you are designing a project?

There is a resultant language in architecture that develops as I design. When I look back at many of our projects, there is consistently an interest with light, but I don't think it's about light per se—it's about a desire to create experiences that are memorable, about having a sensory experience with the architecture.

As a result of that, I utilize whatever is at my disposal to manipulate spaces, and light is something that is just so powerful. I use light as I use other materials and other architectural systems that allow me to develop a very sensory experience. I am interested in an architecture that is ethereal, that feels light, and therefore light is important.

Since early in your career, you've been fascinated with materials. Is there any one material that has captured your attention?

No, but I do like contrasts and I often work with materials that are contrasting. I also like systems that are contrasting—a very solid material or construction system versus a very light material or construction system. I'm constantly looking for new materials that will allow me to achieve what I envision.

Is the tension between opacity and transparency in your projects an innate talent?

This tension stems from the fact that I am interested in heightening the perception of spaces, which includes a person's love of and memory of those spaces. The interplay of the opaque and transparent is one way to accomplish this through contrast. For example, I might have two parallel stone walls that thrust out into a garden, which are then defined or connected by a very light glass wall. It immediately creates a situation that connects the garden and the interior space, creating a memorable, lasting experience.

How has the lineage of early modernism influenced your process and sensibilities?

I think that I have definitely been influenced by the modernist traditions of having an organizing system, of having strong order, and of having a rigorous framework that allows me to develop a project. That is something that I continued to be influenced by after college when I worked with Richard, due to his insistence on having a very rigorous ordering system to organize each project.

It's also something that infuses my architecture as a result of working with Mark Hampton, who was part of the Sarasota School. He had worked with Rudolph and was extremely rational and rigorous in the way that he developed his projects, down to the very minute details. I think those experiences have definitely shaped my work and have affected the way that I develop projects.

Do you sketch?

At the beginning of a project, I often sketch ideas; and then as we're developing the project, I sketch continuously, especially details and thoughts on relationships.

How important is travel to your creative process?

I think it's extremely important. Not only does it allow me to understand what's happening globally, it opens my mind to other cultures and other constructs. Travel also gives me distance. I find that I can think very clearly when I'm in an airplane simply because I'm in an isolated position and know that I will be there for a few hours. A recent trip to China and Tibet, especially Lhasa, made a significant impact on me because there was an otherworldly quality to the urban spaces there that I had never experienced anywhere else.

Does this type of experience inform your work?

I believe we register influences subconsciously and that they surface whenever there is something that triggers them. It's not that I saw any one thing there that I wanted to bring back and immediately use in my work; it is simply that experiences like these create a series of layers in memory that are available to use when we need them.

← MANY OF GONZÁLEZ'S INTERIOR DETAILS CREATE EXPERIENCES WITH LIGHT.

↓ GONZÁLEZ'S FASCINATION WITH MATERIALS IS EVIDENT IN THIS MUSEUM INSTALLATION, WHICH INCLUDED 1,700 LINEAR FEET OF POLYETHYLENE FOAM.

PALM BEACH HOUSE, 1997

Palm Beach, Florida

González updated and reconfigured the interiors of this landmarked 18,000-square-foot Streamline Moderne house, originally designed by Maurice Fatio in 1936. He also designed a beachside living pavilion, a covered poolside terrace, and a series of cascading garden stairs and fountains for the property—all inspired by the site, which is a two-acre parcel of land on the Atlantic Ocean.

↑ UTOPIAN FLORIDIAN LIVING CONDITIONS, WHICH FATIO REFERENCED FOR THE ORIGINAL DESIGN, WERE REINTERPRETED BY GONZÁLEZ TO BRING THE NATURAL BEACH ENVIRONMENT INTO A MODERN CONTEXT.

→ THE HORIZONTAL PATTERNING OF OPAQUE, SEMITRANSPARENT, AND TRANSPARENT GLASS COMBINES WITH A STRONG ROOF PLANE TO ORIENT THE EYE TOWARD THE OCEAN.

↓ SITE PLAN [INDEX OF SPACES: 1 ENTRY 2 POOLSIDE PAVILION 3 BEACHSIDE PAVILION 4 EXISTING HOUSE 5 CASCADING GARDENS 6 GARDEN].

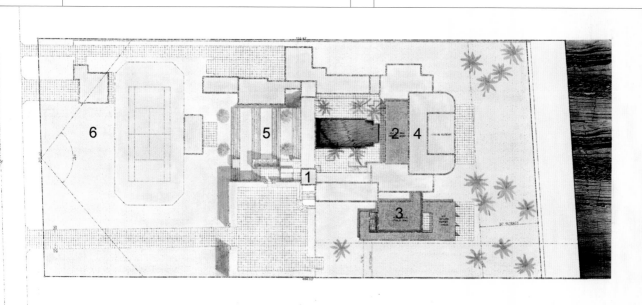

↑ THE SCALE OF THE ARCHITECTURE READS SERENE, A FEELING FURTHERED BY THE REGAL STEPPED-DOWN PARTI PROJECTING TOWARD THE WATER.

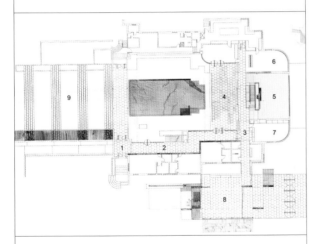

↑ FLOOR PLAN [INDEX OF SPACES: 1 ENTRY TO POOL COURT \ 2 BREEZEWAY \ 3 ENTRY TO HOUSE \ 4 POOLSIDE PAVILION \ 5 LIVING ROOM \ 6 DINING ROOM \ 7 LIBRARY \ 8 BEACHSIDE PAVILION \ 9 CASCADING GARDENS].

← BECAUSE THE ELEMENTAL HOLDS SWAY OVER THE SITE—EXPANSIVE OCEAN VIEWS, A CENTRALLY PLACED POOL, AND AN ABUNDANCE OF SKY—GONZÁLEZ COHESIVELY WOVE THE INTERIOR AND EXTERIOR ROOMS TO ACCENTUATE THE PROPERTY'S NATURAL ATTRIBUTES, AN EXAMPLE OF HIS ABILITY TO CREATE HOLISTIC ARCHITECTURE.

↑ A LINEAR THEME REPEATS AT DIFFERENT SCALES ON THE SITE, AND A VARIETY OF PATTERNS AND HIGHLY TACTILE MATERIALS WERE USED TO DEFINE THE PROJECT'S RELATIONSHIP WITH ITS SETTING.

DESIGN MATTERS MUSEUM INSTALLATION, 2000

Miami, Florida

This Museum of Contemporary Art exhibition evaluated design trends in America. Within its 6,000 square feet of space, 1,700 linear feet of polyethylene foam was bent around 160 fluorescent tubes and 66 chiseled blocks of foam. González chose the polyethylene material because, though ordinary, it is sexy and light, and the staff could use it to repackage the items in the exhibition after it closed.

→ SCALE IS USED TO CREATE A DRAMATIC EFFECT IN THIS MUSEUM INSTALLATION AT MOCA, WHICH GONZÁLEZ DESIGNED AND CURATED FOR THE ARANGO DESIGN FOUNDATION.

↑ THE LIGHT AND MATERIALS GONZÁLEZ USED CREATE AN EPHEMERAL BACKDROP FOR THE DESIGNS FEATURED WITHIN THIS EXHIBITION. THE HIGHLY DETAILED ELEMENTS AND SURPRISING USE OF INNOVATIVE MATERIALS ELEVATE THE MUNDANE TO THE REMARKABLE.

↑ A SEDUCTIVE SENSE OF MYSTERY WAS HEIGHTENED BY THE DESIGN OF THE BACKDROP AND THE SKILLFUL PLACEMENT OF THE DIFFUSED LIGHTING.

→ THE DESIGN OF THE BACKDROP FOR THE EXHIBITION REQUIRED A BALANCING ACT OF STRONG ELEMENTS THAT WERE DYNAMIC WITHOUT BEING OBTRUSIVE.

↑ POLYETHYLENE FOAM SOFTLY BENDS AROUND STANDARD FLUORESCENT TUBES TO DIFFUSE LIGHT AND CREATE AN OTHERWORLDLY ATMOSPHERE.

← THIS TREND-SPOTTING EXHIBITION TURNED INTO A TREND-SETTING ONE AS A RESULT OF GONZÁLEZ'S DRAMATIC INSTALLATION.

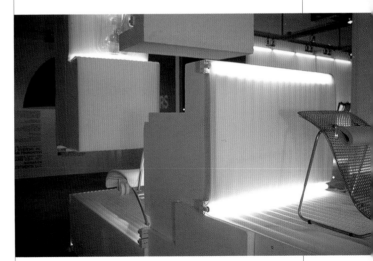

↑ THE VERTICAL LAYERS OF ROLLED FOAM CREATED TRANSLUCENT ARTIFICIAL "SKINS" IN THE SPACE, PRESENTING ONLY GLIMPSES OF THE OBJECTS THEY HELD FROM CERTAIN ANGLES.

KARLA CONCEPTUAL EVENT EXPERIENCES, 2004

Miami, Florida

The owners of this company, which produces bold, innovative events and creates uniquely inventive floral arrangements, asked González to create a design for the 12,000-square-foot converted warehouse that would reflect the company's aesthetic. Achieving their desires, he created a silky, luminous backdrop for KARLA, which garnered him a National AIA Honor Award for Interior Architecture in 2006.

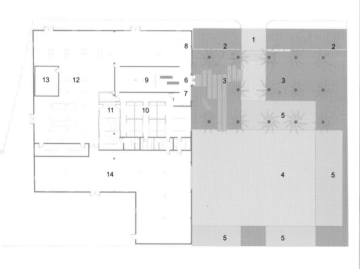

← FLOOR PLAN [INDEX OF SPACES: 1 MAIN ENTRY/DRIVEWAY \ 2 CORTEN STEEL WALL \ 3 GARDEN \ 4 OUTDOOR EVENT SPACE \ 5 PARKING \ 6 ENTRY/LOBBY \ 7 RECEPTION DESK \ 8 CHANGING INSTALLATION \ 9 CONFERENCE ROOM \ 10 OFFICE SPACE \ 11 EXECUTIVE OFFICE \ 12 PRODUCTION STUDIO \ 13 FLOWER COOLER \ 14 WAREHOUSE SPACE].

↑ FLANKED BY ROYAL PALMS AND BAMBOO, KARLA IS NESTLED INTO A LANDSCAPED GARDEN THAT IS AN EXTENSION OF THE INTERIORS.

→ THOUGH THE DEMANDS OF THE COMPANY REQUIRED A NUMBER OF LARGE-SCALE ROOMS AND UTILITARIAN BREVITY, THE SCALE OF EVEN THE MOST SUBSTANTIAL SPACES IS INFUSED WITH A TRANQUIL SENSE OF PROPORTION.

↓ ACRYLIC PANELS DIFFUSE FLUORESCENT LIGHTING THAT WAS PLACED WITHIN THEM TO CREATE A HIGHLY EXPERIENTIAL SPACE.

↓↓ A TRANSLUCENT WALL OF LIGHT INFUSES THE RECEPTION AREA WITH LUMINOSITY. THE TEXTURAL WALLPAPER AND THE GLOSSY SHEEN OF THE EPOXY FLOOR ADD A SUBTLE COMPLEXITY TO THE MONOCHROMATIC COLOR SCHEME OF THE SPACE.

↑ THE SERENITY OF EACH MONOCHROMATIC SPACE IS INTERRUPTED ONLY BY INTERMITTENT INTRODUCTIONS OF CONTRASTING NATURAL MATERIALS.

← THE SCALE OF THE LIT-FROM-WITHIN WALL IN THE LOBBY AREA MAKES A GRAND STATEMENT. A SUBTLE ALTERING OF PATTERN IN THE LUMINESCENT PANELS CREATES ARCHITECTURAL INTEREST.

→ IN THE COURTYARD ENTRY, SUBTLE SHIFTS IN THE PATTERNING OF THE POURED CONCRETE SLABS, TREATED WITH A ROCK-SALT FINISH, CONTRASTS WITH THE RIGOROUS PLACEMENT OF THE ARCHITECTURAL FENESTRATIONS.

PAGES 116–117

→ THE OFFICE AREA IS SPA-LIKE WITH ITS INFUSION OF THE ELEMENTAL. FURTHERING THE BUOYANT FEEL OF THE SPACE, CURLING LEAVES FLOAT IN ACRYLIC BOXES.

→→ THE CONFERENCE ROOM IS DRENCHED IN THE MUTED FLUORESCENT LIGHT THAT EMANATES FROM THE FULL-HEIGHT ACRYLIC PANELS.

CISNEROS FONTANALS ART FOUNDATION (CIFO), 2005

Miami, Florida

CIFO is a nonprofit organization founded by Ella Fontanals-Cisneros in 2002 to promote emerging and multidisciplinary contemporary artists from Latin America. In this burgeoning area of downtown Miami, austere industrial buildings, many of them warehouses, proliferate, so humanizing the 15,000-square-foot museum building within this context was the driving force behind the project. González accomplished this by creating a bamboo tropical forest—with tiles on the facade and plantings in the courtyard. González's firm won an Award of Excellence for this project from the Miami Chapter of the AIA.

↓ THE FACADE OF THE BUILDING WAS COVERED WITH OVER ONE MILLION MULTICOLORED BISAZZA GLASS TILES.

→ THE STRONG SOUTH FLORIDA LIGHT ILLUMINATES THE SKIN OF THE BUILDING, INTENSIFYING THE JUNGLE.

↑ AN ADJACENT PLAZA PLANTED INTERMITTENTLY WITH WEEPING FICUS
AND BAMBOO SEGUES FROM THE URBAN JUNGLE TO THE NATURAL JUNGLE
WITH GEOMETRIC RIGOR.

→ THE HIGHLY COMPLEX DESIGN OF THE FACADE INFUSES THE COMMAND-
ING HORIZONTAL PROFILE OF THE BUILDING WITH VERTICALITY, GROUNDING
THE BUILDING TO ITS SITE.

↑ THE PATTERNING OF THE TILED FACADE TELESCOPES AND DISSOLVES
WITH A SHIFT IN PERSPECTIVE AS THE VIEWER MOVES FROM UP CLOSE TO
FAR AWAY.

↑ FLOOR PLAN [INDEX OF SPACES: 1 BAMBOO GARDEN/PARKING AREA \
2 ENTRY \ 3 RECEPTION \ 4 EXHIBITION SPACE \ 5 CONFERENCE ROOM \ 6 ART
RECEIVING \ 7 STORAGE \ 8 RESTROOMS].

← IN THE INTERIORS OF THE BUILDING, DESIGNED AS A MACHINE FOR
DISPLAYING ART, AN INTERPLAY OF HONEST MATERIALS AND ABUNDANT
LIGHT FORM A SUBDUED BACKDROP FOR THE EXHIBIT.

→ THE GALLERIES SHOW A SPATIAL DEXTERITY THAT HAS EVERYTHING TO
DO WITH CONTEXT.

MUSEUM OF CONTEMPORARY ART
LOBBY RENOVATION, 2006

Miami, Florida

To update the lobby of the museum, which was originally designed by Gwathmey Siegel & Associates, González simplified the spaces and defined a new entry into the museum shop. Evocative of the louvers used in tropical climates, the lattice system he designed creates an ambiguous exterior-like environment linking the entry plaza and the courtyard.

↑ GONZÁLEZ UTILIZES MATERIALS IN UNEXPECTED WAYS TO CREATE DRAMATIC EFFECTS IN HIS ARCHITECTURE.

↑ BLURRING THE LINES BETWEEN THE OUTSIDE AND THE INSIDE,
THE LATTICE CREATES A SUBTLE TEXTURAL LAYERING IN ITS GEOMETRIC
SIMPLICITY.

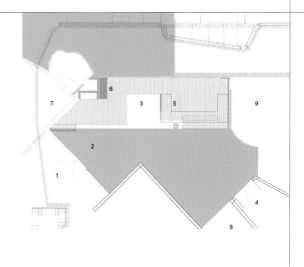

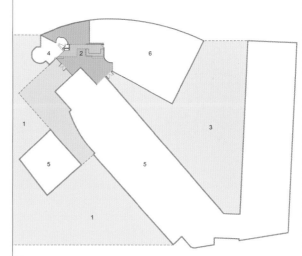

↑↑ BECAUSE THE LATTICE WAS INSTALLED IN A CONTINUOUS BAND, IT READS AS IF IT IS CARVING SPACES WITHIN SPACES.

↑ THE FURNISHINGS FOR THE RENOVATED AREAS WERE WRAPPED WITH LATTICE, PROVIDING TEXTURAL CONTINUANCE.

↑↑ FLOOR PLAN [INDEX OF SPACES: 1 ENTRY PLAZA \ 2 ENTRY \ 3 NEW LOBBY \ 4 COURTYARD \ 5 RECEPTION \ 6 BENCH \ 7 MUSEUM STORE \ 8 GALLERY \ 9 OFFICES].

↑ SITE PLAN [INDEX OF SPACES: 1 ENTRY PLAZA \ 2 NEW LOBBY \ 3 COURTYARD \ 4 MUSEUM STORE \ 5 GALLERY \ 6 OFFICES].

↑ THE SUBTLE ARCING, WRAPPING, AND FLOATING OF THE LATTICE MAKES IT APPEAR TO BE IN A CONSTANT STATE OF FLUX.

INDIAN CREEK HOUSE (2010 projected)

Indian Creek Island, Florida

This 20,000-square-foot house was designed for a two-acre bayfront parcel of land. The architecture was inspired by, captures, filters, and reflects the radiant Miami sun and the city's introspective moon, which are reflected everywhere in the surrounding South Florida waters. González achieved this elemental acuity after a careful reading of the expansive views of Biscayne Bay, and the play of shadows and light that influence the site.

↓ A SKETCH OF THE HOME NESTLED INTO ITS GROVE OF PALMS SUGGESTS ITS STRONG RELATIONSHIP TO NATURE.

→ AND VISUALLY CONNECTED TO THE GARDENS. THE OUTDOOR LIVING ROOMS ARE ENCLOSED WITH WOOD LOUVERS AND GLASS THAT FILTER LIGHT.

↑↑ CANTILEVERED ROOF PLANES CREATE A SERIES OF SPACES THAT
ACT AS SHELTER WHILE FREEING INTERIOR VIEWS FROM INTERRUPTION.

↑ A LAYERING OF SPACES DIVIDED BY SOLID MAHOGANY WINDOW SYSTEMS
OFFERS UNINTERRUPTED VIEWS TOWARD BISCAYNE BAY WHILE CREATING
A SERIES OF SENSATIONS THAT RELATE TO THE HOME'S CONTEXT.

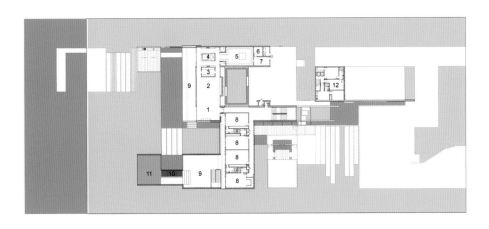

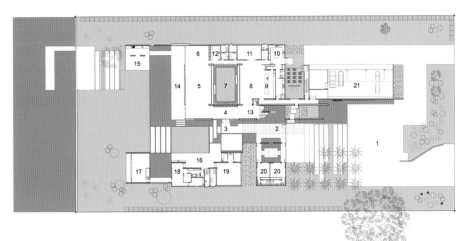

↑↑ SECOND-FLOOR PLAN [INDEX OF SPACES: 1 OFFICE \ 2 MASTER BEDROOM \
3 HIS CLOSET \ 4 MASTER BATHROOM \ 5 HER CLOSET \ 6 ART STORAGE \
7 PANIC ROOM \ 8 BEDROOM \ 9 TERRACE \ 10 JACUZZI \ 11 ROOFTOP LAWN \
12 MAID'S QUARTERS].

↑ GROUND-FLOOR PLAN [INDEX OF SPACES: 1 AUTO COURT \ 2 BREEZEWAY \
3 ENTRY COURT \ 4 FOYER \ 5 LIVING ROOM \ 6 DINING ROOM \ 7 BREAKFAST
COURTYARD \ 8 FAMILY ROOM \ 9 FAMILY KITCHEN \ 10 CATERING KITCHEN \
11 LIBRARY \ 12 WINE BAR \ 13 STAIRS \ 14 LIVING TERRACE \ 15 CABANA \
16 OUTDOOR LIVING \ 17 EXERCISE ROOM \ 18 SPA \ 19 MEDIA ROOM \ 20 GUEST
PAVILION \ 21 SEVEN-CAR GARAGE].

UNIDAD OF MIAMI BEACH (2010 projected)

Community Senior Center

The UNIDAD Community Center was designed to be a sensitive neighbor to a historic 1960s band-shell auditorium located in the same oceanfront park. It was also meant to be a beacon for the community. Contrasting the band shell, the center is a low, horizontal building that quietly makes references to the mid-century elements of its context.

→ CLAD IN PERFORATED PANELS THAT EVOKE THE POROUS QUALITIES OF THE DECORATIVE GRILLE-BLOCKS USED IN THE NEARBY BAND SHELL, THE CENTER MAKES REFERENCE TO ITS MID-CENTURY DESIGN ROOTS.

PROJECTS

← THE PANELS WILL BE ILLUMINATED AT NIGHT AND, LIKE FIREFLIES, WILL
FILL THE PARK WITH KINETIC DOTS OF LIGHT.

↑↑ SECOND-FLOOR PLAN [INDEX OF SPACES: 1 MULTIPURPOSE SPACE \
2 TERRACE \ 3 CATERING KITCHEN].

↑ GROUND-FLOOR PLAN [INDEX OF SPACES: 1 PARK ENTRANCE \
2 BEACH ENTRANCE \ 3 RECEPTION \ 4 MULTIPURPOSE SPACE \ 5 OFFICES \
6 EXECUTIVE OFFICE \ 7 BEACHFRONT TERRACE \ 8 STAIRS \ 9 ROCK GARDEN].

KEY BISCAYNE HOUSE (unrealized)

Key Biscayne, Florida

Sophisticated clients with modern sensibilities drove the design of this 10,000-square-foot residence. They asked González to create a home that would be extraordinarily in tune with nature. To achieve this, the architect used advanced material technology and a celebration of water views to heighten the building's relationship with its surroundings. This design received an Award of Excellence from the Miami Chapter of the AIA.

↓ A CONCEPTUAL SKETCH OF THE HOME'S LONGITUDINAL SECTION.

→ THE DESIGN OF THIS LOFTLIKE RESIDENCE IS A CELEBRATION OF ITS NATURAL SURROUNDINGS. A CURTAIN WALL OF GLASS INTERACTS WITH BOLD, ABSTRACT GEOMETRY TO SIMULTANEOUSLY OFFER REFUGE FROM AND ACCESS TO NATURE.

Camargo Residence   2.7.02

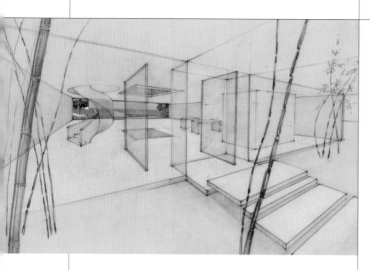

← A CONCEPTUAL SKETCH OF THE HOUSE SHOWING A VIEW THROUGH THE LIVING ROOM OUT TO THE BAY.

↓ PARALLEL WALLS CREATE A DYNAMIC CONDITION THAT LEADS THE EYE DIRECTLY THROUGH THE HOUSE AND OUT TO THE VIEW.

→ THE MEDITATIVE POOL IN THE CENTER OF THE HOUSE IS POSITIONED DIRECTLY BELOW A LIGHT CHAMBER MADE OF LIGHT-SENSITIVE, DICHROIC GLASS THAT SHIFTS IN HUE AND INTENSITY AS IT REFLECTS THE PROGRESSION OF NATURAL SUNLIGHT.

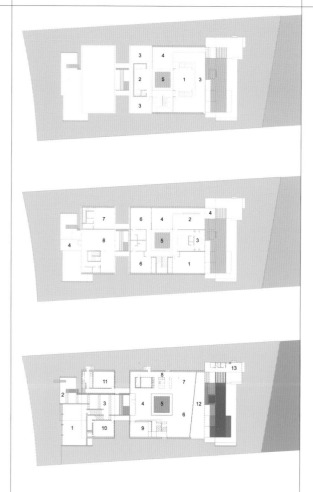

↑→ RENDERINGS DEPICT THE SHIFTING HUES OF LIGHT AT DIFFERING TIMES OF THE DAY.

↑ THIRD-FLOOR PLAN [INDEX OF SPACES: 1 OFFICE \ 2 PAINTING STUDIO \ 3 TERRACE \ 4 TERRACE BELOW \ 5 SKYLIGHT].

↑ SECOND-FLOOR PLAN [INDEX OF SPACES: 1 HER SUITE \ 2 HIS SUITE \ 3 MASTER BATH \ 4 TERRACE \ 5 LIGHT CHAMBER \ 6 BEDROOM \ 7 MAID'S ROOM].

↑ GROUND-FLOOR PLAN [INDEX OF SPACES: 1 GARAGE \ 2 ENTRY GARDEN \ 3 ENTRY COURT \ 4 FOYER \ 5 MEDITATIVE POOL AND LIGHT CHAMBER \ 6 LIVING ROOM \ 7 DINING ROOM \ 8 KITCHEN \ 9 MEDIA ROOM \ 10 EXERCISE ROOM \ 11 STUDIO \ 12 POOL TERRACE \ 13 CABANA].

RON-ROJAS HOUSE (unrealized)

Key Biscayne, Florida

The living spaces in this 5,000-square-foot house were developed in response to the environment in order to allow the homeowner to engage the natural elements surrounding the home in altering degrees of interaction. The experiences vary from being out of doors in a vertical space, which is uncovered and has high walls of clay louvers, to one that is horizontal and surrounded by glass doors that can be opened to breezeways and pools.

→ WRAP-AROUND TERRACES FLOAT OVER POOLS THAT SURROUND THE HOME. ON THE SECOND FLOOR, VIEWS FROM ROOMS AND TERRACES ARE COMPOSED WITH HORIZONTAL OPENINGS.

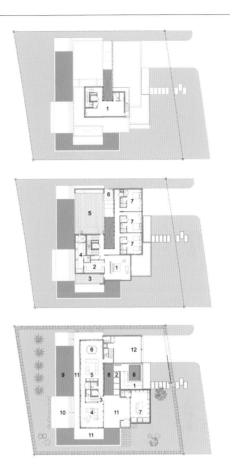

← THE POOLS ARE THE PRINCIPAL ORGANIZING ELEMENTS IN THIS HOME, ORCHESTRATING THE SPACES AND PROVIDING A COOL CONTRAST TO MIAMI'S STRONG LIGHT.

↑↑↑ THIRD-FLOOR PLAN [INDEX OF SPACES: 1 PLAYROOM].

↑↑ SECOND-FLOOR PLAN [INDEX OF SPACES: 1 MASTER BEDROOM \ 2 DRESSING ROOM \ 3 TERRACE \ 4 MASTER BATH \ 5 COVERED TERRACE \ 6 JACUZZI \ 7 BEDROOM \ 8 GUEST SUITE].

↑ GROUND-FLOOR PLAN [INDEX OF SPACES: 1 ENTRY \ 2 ENTRY COURT \ 3 FOYER \ 4 LIVING ROOM \ 5 KITCHEN \ 6 DINING ROOM \ 7 LIBRARY/GUEST ROOM \ 8 REFLECTING POOL \ 9 POOL \ 10 POOL DECK \ 11 TERRACE \ 12 GARAGE].

KEYS RETREAT (unrealized)

The Florida Keys

This design for a spiritual retreat in the Florida Keys explores architecture's potential to be experiential. Through apparatuses, a wall constructed of wood and metal is transformed, allowing a plane of leaves and light to form a new enclosure. This project also illustrates González's use of opacity and transparency to create tension, and it includes manipulations of color, light, and space that parallel a series of sensations.

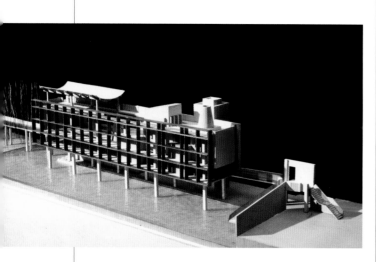

↑ THIS PROJECT MAKES THE MOST OF A CONNECTION BETWEEN LAND AND SEA, AND IT HAS AN ENERGIZING TENSION BETWEEN OPACITY AND TRANSPARENCY. THE SENSORY IS EVOKED THROUGH A PERSON'S INTERACTION WITH THE BUILT.

→ A PROXIMITY TO NATURE IS AT THE HEART OF GONZÁLEZ'S BODY OF WORK, DRIVING HIS EXPLORATIONS OF PLACES WHERE THE NATURAL AND THE MAN-MADE WORLDS MEET.

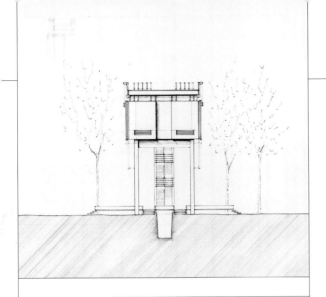

← ELEVATION OF GUEST PAVILION.

↓ THE CURVILINEAR ROOF STRUCTURE PROVIDES A STRONG ICONIC PROFILE AND A POETIC REFERENCE TO THE BUILDING'S NAUTICAL ENVIRONMENT. THE PAVILION'S ROOF STRUCTURE PEELS AWAY AS IF BLOWN UP AT THE EDGES BY THE WIND, RESPONDING TO NATURE'S FORCE WHILE PROVIDING PROTECTION FROM IT.

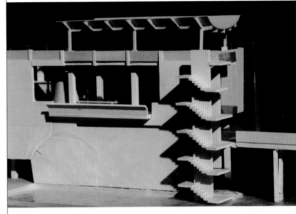

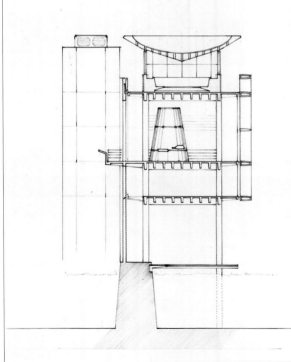

← SECTION THROUGH COMMUNITY BUILDING.

↑ HOVERING ABOVE THE WATER ON PILOTIS, THIS CHAPEL HAS A TENUOUSLY SUSPENDED RAMP, CREATING A PROCESSION THAT TERMINATES AT AN ALTAR THAT OPENS TOWARD THE EASTERN SUNRISE.

CHAD **OPPENHEIM**, NCARB, AIA

Oppenheim Architecture + Design | Miami, Florida

Born in New Hyde Park, New York, in 1971 and raised in the suburbs of New Jersey, Chad Oppenheim was seven years old when he sat in on his first charette.

His parents had decided to build a house, and when the architect came to present his ideas Oppenheim was awestruck by the unfurled plans and the architect's yellow trays and colored pencils. "My parents and I sat around sketching with him," he recalls. "That's when I started drawing houses and thinking that I knew something about architecture!"

Equally influential was a book his mother gave him when he was young. "My mother bought me a Richard Meier book," he remembers. "When I saw the architect's Douglas House on the shores of Lake Michigan, I thought to myself, 'That's what I want to do!'"

As this new fascination took hold, it set him on a trajectory toward a career in architecture. While other boys were looking at Sports Illustrated, Oppenheim read *Architectural Digest*. By the time he was in high school he was taking architecture classes at a local community college. His favorite teacher had attended the Institute for Architecture and Urban Studies, founded by Peter Eisenman, one of the New York Five, and Oppenheim felt an affinity for Eisenman's principles. Before long, he was working in his professor's office after school each day, and by the time he was a junior in high school he had enrolled in a summer exploration program at Cornell University. "I had a rude awakening that

summer," he says. "I realized then that there was so much more to architecture than cool facades!"

Eventually he returned to Cornell as a college student, where he was influenced by the teachings of a number of the Texas Rangers, a group of educators who organized a teaching program at the University of Texas School of Architecture in Austin during the 1950s, and who counted the classical and modern as equally instructive for young architects. During summers, wanderlust took hold. "I would work in a different country every year; first Israel, then Spain and Italy." When he visited Paris, the projects of Le Corbusier drove his pilgrimages. "After seeing practically every Corb project in Paris, I realized the purity in his work," he explains. "His buildings are sturdy because they're built of concrete, but they are sculptural." Ronchamp, he claims, changed his life. "There was so much emotion in Corb's work," he adds, "at times it slipped into the sublime."

Once Oppenheim received his bachelor of architecture degree from Cornell, he accepted a fellowship that took him to Japan, where he worked for a prominent architectural firm for six months. When he returned to the United States, he considered joining firms in Europe and Colorado before signing on with Arquitectonica in Miami.

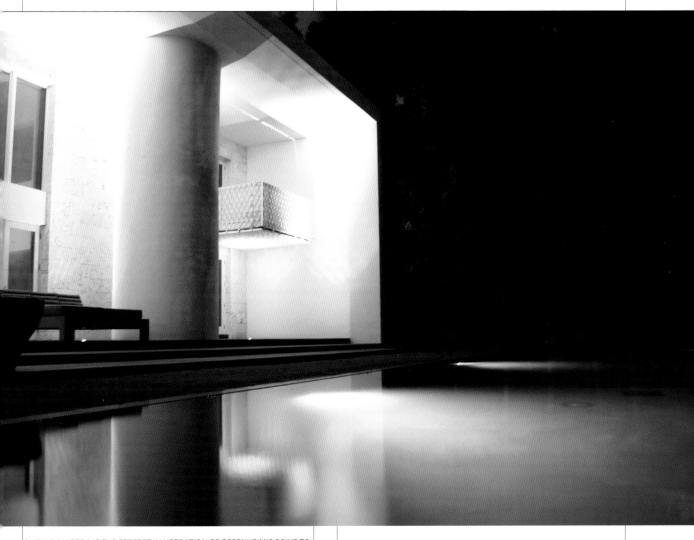

↑ VILLA ALLEGRA IS THE PERFECT ILLUSTRATION OF OPPENHEIM'S DRIVE TO CREATE ARCHITECTURE THAT OFFERS UNIMPEDED ACCESS TO ITS NATURAL SURROUNDINGS.

"I had always been fascinated with the Miami I saw while watching *Miami Vice* with my father when I was young," says Oppenheim. "The other extreme I knew of Florida was my grandmother's retirement community in West Palm Beach. In fact, my image of the state was somewhere between Disney World, *Miami Vice*, and God's waiting room, which turned out to be imprecise!"

It was the buildings featured on *Miami Vice*, which he saw as interesting and playful, that had captured Oppenheim's attention. "When I moved to Miami, I assumed that there would be a liberal attitude toward design," he says. "I had this notion that there was a lack of architectural history in Miami compared to more established cities, so I thought it would be easier to push the envelope."

He did find that Miami's sensibilities were a perfect fit, and in 1999, four years after his arrival, he founded Oppenheim Architecture + Design. "I'm very passionate about architecture," he proclaims. "I would compare it to being in love. When you're in love, everything is enlightened."

ANALYSIS **by Terence Riley, director of the Miami Art Museum, former Philip Johnson Chief Curator of Architecture and Design at the Museum of Modern Art in New York, and founding partner in the architecture firm K/R (Keenan/Riley)**

The recent architecture of Chad Oppenheim demonstrates both the persistence of various tectonic themes rooted in the twentieth century and the increasingly distant cultural and technological divide between then and now.

While virtually all of Oppenheim's projects include lush vegetation—within and without the structure—his architecture presents two distinct modalities, the first that of the city and the second that of a natural or exurban condition. This formal duality is clearly evident in the work of the early moderns as well, but has roots in far earlier times. In his quest to reestablish the classical language of architecture, Andrea Palladio developed contrasting and complementary formal languages for his city palaces and his rural villas.

Le Corbusier's radical visions for high-rise urban living similarly contrast with his reinterpretation of the classic villa in the landscape. As has been well argued by Colin Rowe, Le Corbusier's Villa Savoye can be seen as a formal and spatial restatement of Palladio's grand residential structures in the countryside around Venice.[1] Mies adopts a similar duality, proposing a crystalline, latticelike skyscraper for the city of Berlin at the same time as he proposes a low-lying, concrete structure—sculpted into the earth—as a country house near Potsdam.

A comparison of Oppenheim's Ten Museum Park for downtown Miami and his San Silencio for the Port of Caldera in Costa Rica yields similar results. The residential tower is rendered as a pure, white prismatic exoskeleton, rising above the city and reflecting its underlying grid. Elegantly proportioned, the simple yet refined volumes of the high-rise evoke not just urban conditions but sophisticated urbanity itself. The San Silencio resort project, in contrast, adopts a more organic form, lying low to the ground and outlining the site's natural contours. Through the use of principally natural materials, the structure blends with its surroundings. Like Le Corbusier's sod-roofed rubble-and-log Errázuriz Houses, designed for a country site in Chile, the San Silencio resort consciously evokes a less technological

↑ RILEY COMPARES CAMPUS CENTER TO PETER EISENMAN'S MAX REINHARDT HAUS, DESIGNED FOR BERLIN BUT NEVER BUILT, AND REM KOOLHAAS'S CCTV TOWER, NOW UNDER CONSTRUCTION IN BEIJING.

↑ RILEY SPEAKS OF SAN SILENCIO'S ORGANIC FORM, WHICH LIES LOW TO THE GROUND AND OUTLINES THE SITE'S NATURAL CONTOURS.

and more rustic architectural language than that of the architect's urban projects.

Oppenheim's attitude toward the city, it should be noted, is quite different from Le Corbusier's. The latter saw the city as essentially a problem to be solved and had little sympathy for the urban pleasures that city dwellers love. For instance, he thought sidewalk cafés—the locus of so much Parisian culture—were unhealthy and unsightly. He also believed that listening to the record player at home was far more rewarding—and more sanitary—than attending public concerts. Architecturally, this attitude is reflected in the interiorization of the city in many of his most well known works. An essential element of his conception of the Unité d'Habitation—the "tower in the park" that would become the basic building block for his urban designs—eliminated the life of the street by both isolating the towers from one another and locating commercial space not on the ground floor but on the level above.

Oppenheim's attitude toward the city is much more accepting of the city as it is, whether it be Miami, Las Vegas, or Abu Dhabi. His designs glamorize urban life in seductive

↓ THIS ROOFTOP POOL EXEMPLIFIES HOW OPPENHEIM FRAMES THE EXPERIENTIAL WITH ARCHITECTURE.

renderings that position his projects in the city skyline. Like many projects for private developers, these often create worlds unto themselves, but just as often they make coherent connections to the city's urban fabric.

If Oppenheim's work can be perceived—grosso modo—as adhering to a centuries-long tendency to define architectural distinctions between the city and the country, in other ways his work departs from such well-traveled cultural paths, reflecting various contemporary influences and personal preoccupations. The high-rise Campus Center project for downtown Miami reflects the innovative transformations of tall buildings as first seen in Peter Eisenman's Max Reinhardt Haus, designed for Berlin but never built, and Rem Koolhaas's China Central Television building (the CCTV tower), now under construction in Beijing. Eisenman's project is the first to depart from the polemical position staked out by Adolf Loos in 1922 in his design for the Chicago Tribune tower in Chicago. Loos's design resembled not a tower so much as a gigantic classical column, with base, capital, and fluted shaft.

Eisenman's contribution was to see the skyscraper not as a vertical, centroidal element puncturing the skyline but as a complex form folding in on itself to create a void at its center that is at least as prominent as the structure itself. Koolhaas's CCTV tower and Oppenheim's later design for the Campus Center both achieve the same urban effect: rather than being perceived as a vertical spire, the structures create a horizontal urban axis by framing monumental views of the city. The influence of Koolhaas on Oppenheim and his generation is evident in other projects as well. For example, the precariously composed volumes of Oppenheim's Delano + Mondrian project in Las Vegas recall Koolhaas's similarly conceived Zac Danton project of 1991, designed for Paris. Koolhaas's influence on Oppenheim's generation is more fundamental; however, his seminal work *Delirious New York* has become a how-to manual for recasting contemporary urbanism—so long dominated by Le Corbusier—since it was published in 1978.

Delirious New York also served to revitalize theories of modern architecture for a new generation at a time when the late International Style was the subject of intense criticism by postmodern thinkers. Various projects by Oppenheim, such as the Sonesta Key Biscayne or the Ilona, reflect the broad shift in "post-postmodern" architecture as the surfaces of architecture have begun to assume the importance once associated with architecture's forms.

This position is clearest in the Vokko Headquarters building design for Turkey. The form itself is reduced to a simple rectangular form, whereas the skin is built up in layers—the outer being permeable. The complexity of the surfaces creates a visually rich experience, capturing reflectivity and translucencies that are intermingled with unfiltered vision. Le Corbusier declared that "architecture is the learned game, correct and magnificent, of forms assembled in the light," but Oppenheim and many others of his generation might describe a new game, contingent and transient, of light revealed by surfaces.[2]

Another shared concern of the post-postmodern generation is reflected in the sustainable energy measures and other aspects of "green" architecture seen in Oppenheim's work. Smoke-belching chimneys were once (and in some places still are) accepted symbols of progress and modernity; the challenge facing Oppenheim's generation

↑ THE MARINA + BEACH VILLAGE WAS DESIGNED FOR A COMPETITION IN THE UNITED ARAB EMIRATES.

is to imagine an architecture that offers the comforts and amenities associated with mechanical devices—heated and cooled air, elevators, household appliances, and so forth—while consuming considerably less energy.

Many, if not most, of these green strategies have no objective architectural expression. Rather, often the most visible sign of contemporary green architecture, including Oppenheim's, is the literal presence of planted material within and without the structure. Like the media walls and machine metaphors that served as expressions of the aspirations of earlier generations of architects, the integration of biological systems within architecture's structural and me-

chanical systems—as seen in Oppenheim's UAE project—is an emblem of a new sensibility.

Oppenheim's work also frankly embraces the sensual, if not hedonistic, side of life in subtropical South Florida and Las Vegas—the sites of many of his projects—and elsewhere. Images of his houses, residential towers, resorts, and hotels show toned bodies relaxing amid limpid pools of water, tropical gardens, and extravagant, flowing spaces bounded by lush architectural surfaces. These images can be hard to reconcile with the thrift-minded energy use of sustainable architecture, but that contradiction represents the challenges facing the current generation of architects.

↑↑ PARCEL D WAS OPPENHEIM'S SUBMISSION FOR A SUSTAINABLE COMPETITION IN SAN JUAN, PUERTO RICO.

↑ THIS RENDERING OF THE LOBBY AREA OF SAN SILENCIO IN COSTA RICA ILLUSTRATES OPPENHEIM'S BLENDING OF ARCHITECTURE AND ITS NATURAL SURROUNDINGS.

If what is commonly called commercial architecture is going to play a significant role in shaping our cities, it needs to address more issues than short-term profitability, not the least of which is energy usage. Whether or not new technologies can be developed to meet this challenge is unclear. But Oppenheim's work is a sign that the current generation of architects is devoting considerable talent and effort to the cause.

Saxon Henry: You have remarked about an emotional push/ pull you experience between the built and the natural world. How does this inform your creative process?

I guess it depends on where I'm working. When I'm designing a project in a potent natural environment, I want to respect that environment as much as possible. I'm always in awe of the beauty of nature so I feel that it's difficult to actually create something more beautiful than nature. I like to let the natural surroundings infuse our projects and become the star of the show.

For instance, with San Silencio in Costa Rica, the idea was to have the architecture blend seamlessly with nature, to disrupt nature as little as possible by minimizing the mass and the experience of the architecture. In a sense, we're letting the architecture frame the natural world, which I believe is why people want to go to Costa Rica. Our work is to unlock the power and the beauty of a particular site. This concept could obviously be transformed into an urban setting as well, but I think it's more potent in a natural setting of great drama.

When I was designing San Silencio, I sat on this cliff overlooking the jungle and it was like a dream. I thought to myself, I don't want to build anything: I just want to sit here and enjoy. I've always tried to build as little as possible and to do the minimum to achieve the maximum, and I'm also a romantic, so the natural projects are about the free elements—the trees, the sky, the water.

Another example of this is a project in the Turks and Caicos where we orientated a village similar to the way ancient civilizations would have worked with the movement of celestial bodies. I think this is important because we have become somewhat removed from the natural world with all of the technology we have in our lives. For this project, we are letting the natural environment create orientations and dictate where we are placing buildings. This is similar to how the ancient art of geomancy or Asian principles would dictate how to locate a project.

In a natural setting, this is one of the challenges—how do you locate architecture? We try to work with the natural forces, like the movement of the sun and the moon, as we try to capitalize on the beauty surrounding the buildings. In this sense, the natural world actually becomes one of the materials that we work with. There are physical materials but there are also metaphysical and ethereal materials, such as the sky, the light, the weather, the reflections, and the greenery—all of those things to me are my main ingredients for a project set in nature. I believe the architecture is there only to allow one to appreciate these elements.

Has this level of considering contexts always informed your work?

Yes, and the arduous creative process we undertake to understand the context in which we're working is multidimensional. When I studied at Cornell, everything was heavily driven by context, and that could mean the physical context, a sociological context, or a financial context. There are so many layers of context. That said, we most typically start with a deep understanding of and a deep investigation of the physical context.

Some of this comes from research and the resulting imagery that we find. When we go to a site, we try to listen to the land and understand it. I'm very much a lover of great skies, and when dealing with a primitive and elemental beauty, we try to remove ourselves from the notion of form and build from the notion of experience. This is the place from which we like to create. We are determined not to think about form but merely to let the experience of a place derive the form. It's a more romantic version of form follows function, which I would call form follows experience.

How does your creative process unfold as you begin a project?

Usually I begin by grabbing all of these ingredients that I like. In fact, I want to grab as many ingredients as possible, and many of them are ethereal experiences. I usually have many ideas: I want to create this or that feeling; I want to make sure that from this room you have this amazing sunset and from here you can watch the sunrise or interact with a reflecting pool, for example.

I wouldn't say that I know what I'm envisioning early on, but I have all of these loose ideas or flashes, and then little by little a project starts to become more formalized. It's almost like gelatin, which has to harden. As it's hardening, I'm manipulating it. This is an arduous process during which we prefer to let the look of a project be discovered as opposed to deciding how it will look and then supporting it with research afterwards. It's an exploratory process, almost like archaeology. We are uncovering the project from the earth and piecing together clues until eventually we put something together that works.

One of the things I always have to be careful about is that I don't have so many ingredients that they fight with each other. You really need the "big" idea. I tend to be incredibly excited, and I can come up with a million ideas, so I have to actually make sure that I don't overindulge and put too many ingredients in the mix! There are many layers to each project and there are simply so many details, but as far as I'm concerned, asking how people are going to experience the architecture is the final endgame. A project can look great in renderings, but at the end of the day, how does it sound, how does it smell, how does it feel on a multidimensional, sensory level? Those are the vital questions.

In his essay, Riley observes that you have a worldly side to you and that you approach work with many preoccupations. Would you say that's true?

Yes, and that's why my work is experientially driven. I've been fortunate to have had the opportunity to travel extensively around the world. In my architectural education, I've been able to study and work in many different countries. Because travel has afforded me the opportunity to see what doesn't work, I realized early on that something may look great in a drawing or in a model, but when it's translated into architecture, it fails. Though there are certainly many reasons projects fail, and an architect doesn't always have complete control of a project, I think the reason for many failures is that the humanistic aspects of architecture are put on the back burner. I believe architecture should be about enhancing the way people live and the way people appreciate the world that we live in.

I feel that this enhancement of the human condition is my number-one preoccupation. This includes pleasure and beauty, which most people would likely consider shallow concepts in the world of architecture. But I feel that if you deal with the emotions of pleasure, beauty, and delight, you begin to define an architecture in which those feelings are imbued.

You speak of that moment when you saw the tools of the architect at seven years of age as defining. Why do you think that experience was such a revelation?

It was because the experience was about dreaming. I just returned from a trip during which I was master-planning a city for 150,000 people in the Middle East. During the initial meetings, I challenged everyone to dream, to put the realities on the back burner and come up with something that is so phenomenal, so wonderful, and so magical that nothing can limit the thinking behind the project. This attitude stems from that experience of sitting around that table when I was seven while my parents dreamed the ideas that would infuse our new home.

My parents were quite young and inexperienced at that time, and they had an open attitude. For me it was an interesting process to see the way those dreams and ideas were translated from the imagination into a reality. That's why the experience was such a potent one. Now I find myself asking, "What is the most wonderful thing you can dream up?" Then I say, "Let's build it!" I see this as a strong undertone in our work, which I call fantasy optimism.

↑ THE LONG HOUSE ON MUSTIQUE ISLAND IN THE GRENADINES IS MEANT TO NESTLE INTO THE EXOTIC BEAUTY OF THE ISLAND.

PAGES 160–161

↓↓ OPPENHEIM ORIENTED THE BUILDINGS WITHIN MANDARIN ORIENTAL'S TREE TOP VILLAS ON DELLIS CAY TO MAKE THEM HIGHLY INTERACTIVE WITH THE CELESTIAL BODIES THAT TRAVERSE THE ISLAND'S SKY.

Do you sketch?

I'm always sketching to try and figure out how I want something to feel, but the process for me is never static. I also might use folded or torn paper to dictate what I'm trying to express, rather than a pencil. There is a project we're working on in Dubai for which I used paper to show how the architecture would be peeling off of the building. I was communicating the notion of building as landscape, and as I began peeling off pieces of the paper the result formed the idea for the design process.

The way we work in our office is that I have a phenomenal team of incredibly talented people on all different levels, and I maintain a studio environment. I guess I'm the head critic and director of design because most of the time I explain the feeling, usually sketching in the moment, and then turn it over to the team to implement. My wife and I were just looking at some sketches from this Dellis Cay project that we're doing for the Mandarin Oriental, and I was in awe of how my team can take these abstract sketches and the words that I'm using and turn them into architecture. It's a very interesting process.

I actually distance myself from the production of the drawings. A professor of mine once told me that I'm a perfectionist when it comes to drawings. It is true: I would sit at the table and draw unending versions of one idea. It is just my nature to get bogged down in a corner or with the simplest line. I could sit for hours and try to figure out different placements for a door! There are so many other ways I can use my energy in a more productive manner. For this reason, it works better for me to have someone doing the drawings while I'm editing, refining, and giving the direction.

I'm always working on at least ten projects at one time, so it would be impossible for me to create the production drawings and the 3-D models. But I do have my hand in every project, whether I'm scribbling over a plan to manipulate the drawings or sketching ideas and photographing images of the site from myriad angles.

In fact, I'm obsessive with photography in terms of capturing details. I have thousands of crude, informative photos that illustrate the mood I want to capture. I'll see a building and photograph it to illustrate the type of metal finish I want or the tone I want the wood to be. It's easier to communicate those things with photography because it is sensory. I even use video to capture the sound of water when that's what I want the architecture to evoke.

Riley drew a parallel to Rem Koolhaas. Did this resonate creatively?

Rem has been a tremendous influence, among many other architects who have inspired me. He actually came to lecture at Cornell when I was in my fifth year, and he was touching upon many things that I had been thinking about. His creativity and his way of looking at things with an open-minded clarity of hyperfunctionality is something that rings true for me.

Is the process of designing a building or project in Florida different than in the Middle East or Las Vegas in terms of natural light?

I had an epiphany about light this past summer when I spent some time in Belgium, where the light quality was amazing.

My wife and I were wearing clothes that matched in Miami, but once we were there the hues of white read as completely different shades! There was something about that incredibly crisp white light that was so revealing, which proves how it differs from place to place. Light can be just as powerful a revelation in architecture, and it is always a critical material when we're designing a project.

In the Middle East, we spend so much time trying to figure out how to take the light off of the glass because it's a source of heat. I've been thinking lately that a celebration of the difference between light and darkness, or the absence of light, is what's important. In Dubai, we created a shaded garden on an incredible scale, which became a place of filtered light. Through working on projects like this, I've actually been transforming my original design criteria of maximizing light and maximizing openness because we're now building in climates where light can be a negative element.

The reason it is so easy to celebrate natural light in South Florida is its qualities, which can be an extraordinarily reflective element in architecture. Now that I've been dealing with more intense light I'm looking to control it and to use it in a more powerful way. Particularly where architecture is concerned, every region of the world has its own dictates when it comes to light. In Costa Rica, for instance, light can take on so many personalities—be it moonlight or sunlight or how the light glows at sunset. It's what light does that's important—the way it flushes a wall or permeates a room with a certain mood.

Has anything about being an architect surprised you in terms of the creative process?

So many things surprise me every day, but not necessarily on a creative level. Of all the layers that we deal with as architects, the creative side is the part that is the most entertaining. There are so many other challenging issues, such as how creativity can be manipulated by the reality of constructability, or how to align creativity with the reality of the built world. It actually defines much of our architecture in that we are constantly exploring how to deal with things in the simplest way, and how to make projects as easy to build as possible given the things that we want to accomplish and the level of the experiential that we want to create.

That battle between affordability and creativity is the thing that surprises me the most. I'm always trying to push the envelope, and I think we're respected for our sense of realism, which is something that makes us desirable for clients who want to explore but also want to make sure that it can be built. I can't underscore enough the arduous nature of the process. It's highly cathartic.

I'm not a person with a great deal of patience, and maybe that's one of the things that drives me—let's call it a refusal to believe that things can't be done. I never have that in my mind; I always say that whatever it takes, we're going to make it happen. I guess it's my childhood optimism, which still exists in me despite the challenges I'm confronted with on an hourly basis. These challenges are inherent in the process of discovery as we push the envelope in order to build and create architecture that doesn't exist on paper.

ILONA, 2003

Miami Beach, Florida

The edifice of this 27,000-square-foot condominium complex makes subtle references to passing cruise ships and its neighborhood's Art Deco style. The material palette is simple and sincere—white stucco, an aluminum glazing system, perforated aluminum panels, and shell-stone details. These connect the building to the local fabric's traditions and techniques. The Miami Chapter of the AIA awarded Oppenheim Unbuilt and Built Merit Awards for Ilona.

→ A SCULPTURAL ENTRY FENCE, AS UNDULANT AS THE WAVES THAT CRASH AGAINST THE PROWS OF SHIPS, MARKS THE BOUNDARY TO THE STREET.

↑ MASSIVE PILOTIS THAT SUPPORT THE STRUCTURE LIFT THE ENTRY TO THE BUILDING FROM GRADE, MAKING THE WALKWAY APPEAR TO HAVE BEEN CARVED FROM THE BUILDING'S MASS.

↑ THIS VIEW OF ILONA ILLUSTRATES THE PARTI OF THE PROJECT, AS THE SHAPE OF THE ELONGATED HEXAGONAL BUILDING AND ITS ROOFTOP ELEMENTS SUBTLY ECHO THE CONTOURS OF CRUISE SHIPS THAT TRAVEL NEARBY WATERS.

↑ ALIGNED WITH THE SUN'S PATH AS IT CROSSES FROM THE OCEAN TO THE BAY, ILONA'S STRUCTURE CONTAINS INTIMATE OUTDOOR SPACES THAT PROVIDE THE EXPERIENTIAL ELEMENT OPPENHEIM ADVOCATES IN ARCHITECTURE.

↓ LOWER TERRACES, ENCLOSED BY ALUMINUM SCREENS, CANTILEVER FROM THE MAIN STRUCTURE TO BECOME AMPLE OUTDOOR ROOMS. THE BRISE-SOLEIL PROVIDES PRIVACY AND ACTS AS A SUN-SCREEN.

→ BOLD MODERN ARCHITECTURE DEMANDS BOLD GESTURES IN FURNISHINGS.

VILLA ALLEGRA, 2004

Miami Beach, Florida

This 9,000-square-foot home, which belongs to Oppenheim and his wife, Ilona, was a nondescript one-story house before the couple renovated it. Oppenheim's intention was to maximize the new home's ability to interact with Miami's tropical climate, and the result is striking. The residence, with its statuesque outdoor spaces, offers the couple an environment within which they can enjoy the lush natural surroundings to the fullest. The Florida Association of the AIA and AIA Miami each awarded Oppenheim a Merit Award of Excellence for this project.

→ A MONUMENTAL VOLUME, CARVED FROM THE REAR FACADE OF THE HOME, FORMS A PARTIALLY PROTECTED SPACE THAT SERVES AS A TRANSITION BETWEEN THE INTERIOR AND EXTERIOR OF VILLA ALLEGRA.

→ → THE ENTRY OF THE HOME HOLDS A REFLECTING POOL THAT ALIGNS WITH A PERFORATION IN THE ROOF TO INFUSE THE SPACE WITH REFLECTED LUMINESCENCE.

↑↑ THE LARGE CIRCULAR COLUMN THAT COMMANDS THE EXPANSIVE OUTDOOR ROOM ON THE HOME'S BACK FACADE CONTAINS A SHOWER THAT IS OPEN TO THE SKY.

↑ THE SECOND FLOOR FEATURES A SECLUDED BALCONY OFF OF THE MASTER BEDROOM, AN EXAMPLE OF OPPENHEIM'S ABILITY TO ZERO IN ON FORM-FOLLOWING-EXPERIENCE OPPORTUNITIES.

↑↑ THE MATERIALLY RICH ENVIRONMENT OF THE ENTRY PAVILION MAKES IT READ AS AN EXTENSION OF ITS NATURAL SETTING.

↑ SURFACES OF WOOD INFUSE THE MASTER BATHROOM WITH SPA-LIKE WARMTH, ILLUSTRATING OPPENHEIM'S ADEPT HANDLING OF NATURAL MATERIALS INDOORS.

↓ ELEVATION.

↓↓ THE HOME HAS A CLEAN, QUIET QUALITY THAT SIGNIFIES MODERN ARCHITECTURE AT ITS BEST. OPPENHEIM CANTILEVERED THE STAIR TREADS IN A MINIMALIST MOVE.

MONTCLAIR, 2005

Miami Beach, Florida

The area of South Beach in which this 65,000-square-foot condominium complex is located brought with it historical preservation restrictions and municipal zoning constraints. The new construction straddles a postwar building that was incorporated into the design. A pleasure garden with an edgeless pool, situated on the top of the historic structure, serves as the complex's main public space. The Florida AIA gave Oppenheim an Honor Award of Excellence for the design of the Montclair, the Miami Chapter presented his firm with an Award of Excellence, and the Miami Design Preservation League recognized the project with a Commercial Renovation Award.

↑↑ TWO NEW FIVE-STORY STRUCTURES WRAP AROUND THE EXISTING TWO-STORY BUILDING, CREATING AN OPEN COURT IN THE SKY.

↑ THE COMPLEX HOLDS FORTY UNITS, SOME NEWLY CREATED AND SOME SET WITHIN THE EXISTING BUILDING. A ROUGH KEYSTONE BASE, MINED LOCALLY, CONTRASTS WITH THE MATERIALS—PRIMARILY GLASS, ALUMINUM, AND STUCCO—OF THE NEW STRUCTURE.

→→ ALUMINUM SCREENS OF VARIED PROPORTIONS AND TRANSPARENCIES ENCIRCLE THE PROJECT IN DISTINCT PATTERNS, CREATING EPHEMERAL MASSES THAT FILTER LIGHT.

↑ THE MONTCLAIR'S LOCATION, ACROSS THE STREET FROM A CIVIC PLAZA, DEMANDED THAT THE POROUS OUTER STRUCTURE PROVIDE PRIVACY.
→ THE ALUMINUM BRISE-SOLEIL CREATES INTIMATE SPACES BUT ALLOWS AMPLE LIGHT AND BREEZES TO WAFT ONTO PRIVATE BALCONIES.

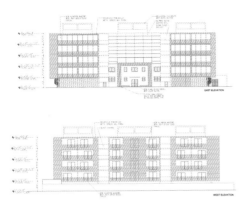

↑ EAST/WEST ELEVATIONS.

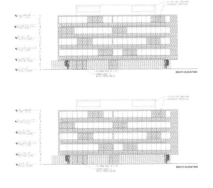

↑ NORTH/SOUTH ELEVATIONS.

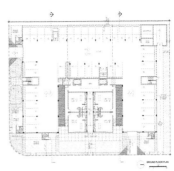

↑ EAST/WEST ELEVATIONS.

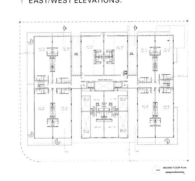

↑ EAST/WEST ELEVATIONS.

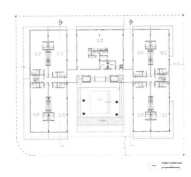

↑ EAST/WEST ELEVATIONS.

ILONA BAY, 2006

Miami Beach, Florida

This 22,000-square-foot condominium complex contains eight four-story town homes and a three-story penthouse with views of Biscayne Bay and the downtown Miami skyline. The meshing of materials includes glass, plastered concrete, and aluminum, orchestrated to blend harmoniously with neighboring structures while eschewing recognizable typological references. Oppenheim's firm won an Unbuilt Design & Honor Award from the Florida AIA for the project.

→ THE MANIPULATIONS OF THE SCALE AND MASSING OF THIS BUILDING ARE EVIDENT IN ITS ARRANGEMENT OF SOLID FORMS AND VOIDS. THE TOPMOST FORM READS LIGHTER AND MORE ETHEREAL THAN THE HEAVIER RECTANGULAR FORM BENEATH IT.

PAGES 180–181

→ THIS DETAIL OF THE BUILDING'S ARCHITECTURAL ELEMENTS SHOWS HOW SUNLIGHT INTERACTS WITH THE PROTRUDING FRAMES TO CREATE A SCULPTURAL EFFECT—THE LIGHT AND THE ABSENCE OF LIGHT, IN SHADOW, ARE THE DEFINING ELEMENTS.

→→ FLOOR-TO-CEILING WINDOWS ARE PUSHED BACK INTO THE MASSING OF THE BUILDING, PROVIDING A SUN SHIELD FOR THE INTERIORS AND ARCHITECTURAL INTEREST ON THE EXTERIOR.

→→→ ILONA BAY'S EXTERIOR IS A RIGOROUSLY COMPLEX SERIES OF FRAMES THAT PROTRUDE FROM AND ARE PUSHED INTO THE BUILDING'S MASSING.

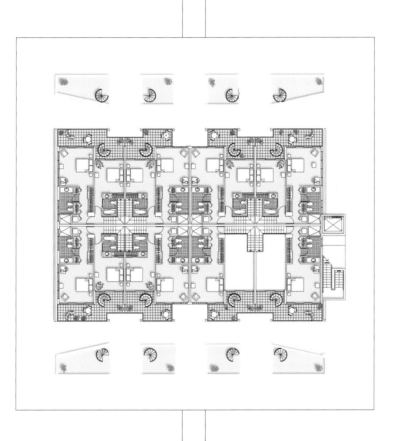

← THE HORIZONTAL WINDOW FENESTRATIONS IN THE SOLID VOLUME ON
THE LOWER FACADE CREATE THE ILLUSION THAT THEY ARE A DESCENDING
CONTINUATION OF THE LONG, THIN PERFORATIONS IN THE ROOF.

↑ FLOOR PLAN.

GALERIE EMMANUEL PERROTIN, 2006

Miami, Florida

This Miami gallery is a satellite of the Parisian gallery of the same name. Design details for the renovated and expanded building include a tiled facade, an exposed post-and-beam structure, and clerestory lighting. The existing structure, built in 1959, was a warehouse with double-height spaces to allow delivery trucks to enter the building—perfect proportions for the creation of expansive walls that now display works of art.

↑ EXPOSED T-BEAMS, A CURVILINEAR MOSAIC STAIR, AND ORIGINAL TERRAZZO FLOORS ARE INTERIOR ELEMENTS IN THE LOBBY OF THE GALLERY, WHICH OPENS TO THE EXHIBITION SPACES BEYOND.

→→ THREE VOLUMES CANTILEVER ON THIS BUILDING. APPEARING TO DEFY GRAVITY, THEY CREATE A DRAMATIC EXTERIOR AND FREE THE INTERIOR SPACES OF STRUCTURAL CONSTRAINTS TO PROVIDE THE IDEAL CONDITIONS FOR VIEWING ART.

↓ A MIX OF TRANSPARENT AND TRANSLUCENT GLASS TEMPERS THE INTENSE NATURAL LIGHT THAT FILTERS INTO THE ENTRY AREA.

↓ THE BIGGEST CHALLENGE FOR OPPENHEIM'S TEAM WAS TO MAINTAIN THE ORIGINAL CHARACTER OF THE SPACES WHILE INTEGRATING THE MECHANICAL SYSTEMS IN AN INCONSPICUOUS MANNER THAT WOULD ALLOW THE MAXIMUM CLEAR WALL SPACE POSSIBLE.

2228 PARK AVENUE, 2006

Miami Beach, Florida

Located in the arts district of Miami Beach, this residential project is nestled among important city buildings, including the Miami City Ballet, the Bass Museum of Art, and the Miami Beach Public Library. The two luxury town homes with enclosed parking spaces and private rooftop pools also have private entry gardens and mid-level verandas. The Florida Association of the AIA and AIA Miami each presented Oppenheim with an Award of Excellence for this modernized version of the brownstone.

↓ THE DESIGN OF THE STRUCTURE WAS DEFINED BY THE RESTRICTIONS OF THE ODDLY SHAPED SITE, WHICH IS BORDERED ON ONE SIDE BY A CANAL.

→ THE VOID ABOVE THE PATTERNED SCREEN REFLECTS THE VOLUMETRICS OF A DYNAMIC NEW MODERN ARCHITECTURE.

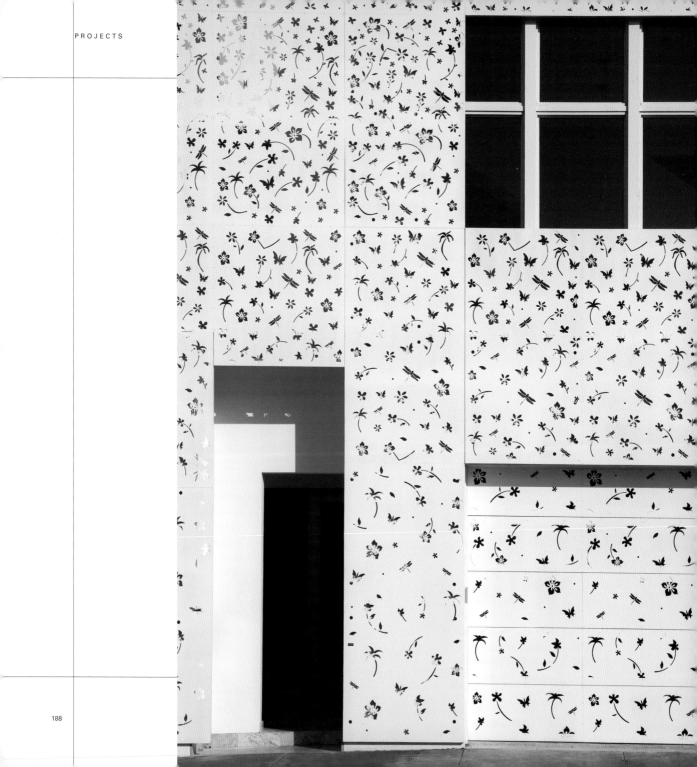

←← A CLOSER VIEW OF THE PATTERNS ON THE SCREEN BRINGS SYMBOLS OF THE LUSH NATURAL ATTRIBUTES OF MIAMI BEACH INTO FOCUS.

← LIGHT WAFTS THROUGH THE SCREEN TO ANIMATE THE FACADE. OPPENHEIM MAINTAINS THAT IT ISN'T LIGHT PER SE BUT WHAT LIGHT DOES THAT INFORMS ARCHITECTURE.

↓ THE FLORAL BRISE-SOLEIL WRAPPING THREE SIDES OF THE BUILDING TAKES ITS INSPIRATION FROM THE BAS-RELIEF ON THE NEIGHBORING HISTORIC BUILDING.

PAGES 190–191

→ THE CUTOUT METAL SHAPES ARE NOT STATIC, REFLECTING THE LIVELY CLIMATE OF THE SETTING.

→→ AS A NOD TO THE BUILDING'S LOCATION WITHIN THE ARTS DISTRICT, AN UNDULANT SCULPTURE WAS WRAPPED AROUND ITS FACADE DURING ART BASEL MIAMI BEACH IN 2007.

TEN MUSEUM PARK, 2007

Miami, Florida

This 600,000-square-foot mixed-use condominium tower rises above Biscayne Bay like a dynamic beacon, the distillation of everything pleasurable about Miami. Oppenheim describes the building as an exploration of the hedonistic possibilities of architecture in a futuristic tropical playground of urban sophistication. The Florida AIA recognized this project with an Award of Excellence.

→ TEN MUSEUM PARK HAS A LINEAR, WELL-PROPORTIONED EXOSKELETON THAT RISES FIFTY STORIES ABOVE THE BAY.

↑ INTERIOR "LIVING MODULES" MAXIMIZE SPATIAL OPENNESS AND EXPANSIVE VIEWS.

↓ THE PARTI FOR THE DESIGN OF BOTH THE PRIVATE AND PUBLIC SPACES WITHIN THE HIGH-RISE WAS FRAMING FRAGMENTS OF WATER, CITY, AND SKY.

↓↓ THE TOWER REFLECTS FLORIDA'S STRONG NATURAL LIGHT AS DAYLIGHT DAWNS, PROGRESSES, AND WANES, PROVING THAT ARCHITECTURE CAN REFLECT NATURE EVEN IN URBAN SETTINGS.

PAGES 194–195

→ THE STRUCTURE, WHICH REFLECTS ITS UNDERLYING GRID, IS ELEGANTLY PROPORTIONED.

→ MIAMI'S SENSUAL BRAND OF MODERNITY IS EVOKED IN TEN MUSEUM PARK'S INTERIORS.

COR (2010 projected)

Oppenheim created this design of COR for a competition. The criterion was to design the first sustainable, mixed-used condominium for downtown Miami. Oppenheim's solution represents a dynamic synergy between architecture, structural engineering, and ecology. Planned for the design district, the project would extract its power from its environment by utilizing the latest advancements in wind turbines, photovoltaic cells, and solar hot-water generation. The Miami Chapter of the AIA awarded Oppenheim's firm an Honorable Mention for Unbuilt projects for its design of COR.

→ OPPENHEIM'S VISION FOR COR WILL RISE FOUR HUNDRED FEET ABOVE THE SURROUNDING CITYSCAPE.

↓ ELEMENTS OF COR'S SUSTAINABILITY FEATURES.

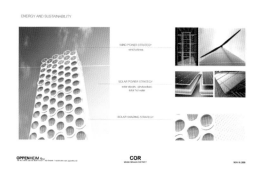

PROJECTS

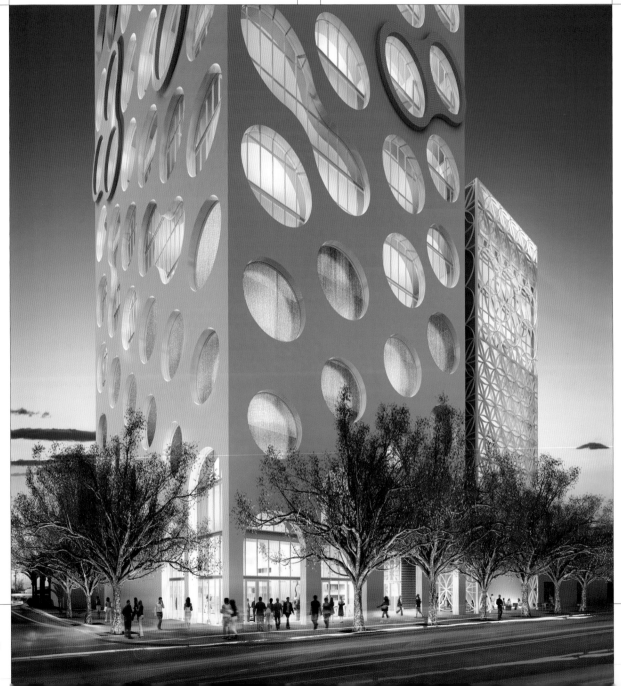

↑ PLAN FOR LEVEL-TWO RETAIL MEZZANINE.

↑ PLAN FOR A RESIDENTIAL UNIT.

↑ SITE PLAN.

↑ THE DESIGN OF COR'S EXOSKELETON SHELL INCORPORATED THE BUILDING'S STRUCTURE, A THERMAL MASS FOR INSULATION, SHADING FOR NATURAL COOLING, AN ENCLOSURE FOR TERRACES, AND ARMATURES FOR TURBINES.

OPPOSITE:
←← THE ECOLOGICAL ASPECTS OF COR, WHICH INCLUDED A HYPER-EFFICIENT EXOSKELETON SHELL, WILL BE INTEGRATED INTO ITS ARCHITECTURAL IDENTITY.

3MIDTOWN (2010 projected)

Miami, Florida

The design of this project, intended for an entire block of midtown Miami, is broken into smaller components to allow for a reduction in perceived mass. The architectural infrastructure creates a harmonious diversity, with tower components that gently twist off axis and out of the way of neighboring views. The Miami AIA gave Oppenheim an Unbuilt Award of Excellence for this project.

→ THE DESIGN, WITH ITS DYNAMIC AND SYSTEMATIC RHYTHM OF SOLID AND VOID ABSTRACTS, IS MONOCHROMATICALLY PRISTINE.

↓ IN THE TIGHT URBAN FABRIC, THE VARIED PATTERNING OF THE ARCHITECTURE OFFERS PRIVACY THROUGH ITS CREATION OF PORCHES, VERANDAS, AND LOGGIAS.

SONESTA BEACH RESORT (2012 projected)

Key Biscayne, Florida

Porous massing, a light footprint, and unencumbered views were the starting points for the design of this 1,700,000-square-foot hotel and condominium project. A new ground plane was created to provide all of the resort's open areas and public spaces with panoramas of the shores of Key Biscayne. This created a subterranean zone where all of the operational requirements could be neatly concealed and efficiently arranged.

→ THE ASSEMBLAGE OF TOWERS HAS RANDOM VARIATIONS THAT RELATE TO THE WATERFRONT CONTEXT.

↓ A TYPICAL FLOOR PLAN FOR A 3,000-SQUARE-FOOT RESIDENCE.

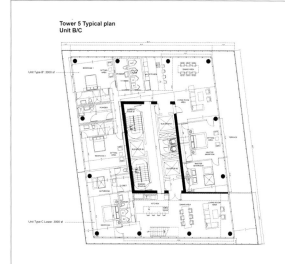

Tower 5 Typical plan
Unit B/C

→ THE BRISE-SOLEIL THAT SKIMS EACH OF THE SIX TOWERS MAINTAINS UNRESTRICTED VIEWS WHILE RESPONDING TO CLIMATIC CONCERNS.

↓ AESTHETICALLY, THE SKIN HYBRIDIZES THE FLORIDA VERNACULAR WHILE REPRESENTING A CONTEMPORARY NOTION OF BREATHABLE FACADES.

MARCO ISLAND MARRIOTT

(2014 projected)

Marco Island, Florida

Because Marco Island is the largest landmass of the Ten Thousand Islands archipelago, it was necessary for Oppenheim to maintain a harmonious equilibrium between nature and the man-made. Another of Oppenheim's intentions was to create architecture with simple gestures that capture the essence and ease of the Gulf Coast Florida lifestyle.

→ FIVE RECTILINEAR VOLUMES OF SIMILAR WIDTH AND DIVERSE PROPORTIONS ARE ARRANGED TO OPTIMIZE BEACH VISTAS.

PAGES 208–209

→ LUSH TROPICAL LANDSCAPING AND POOLS CASCADE TOWARD THE GULF, WEAVING THROUGH THE ARCHITECTURE TO CREATE PROCESSIONAL EXPERIENCES THAT LEAD TO THE WATER'S EDGE.

CAMPUS CENTER (unrealized)

This proposed LEED-certified structure was conceived for a competition sponsored by Miami Dade College. For their entry, Oppenheim and his design team proposed a portal composed of a base and a top, connected by two towers. The design provides expansive exterior public spaces at ground level and in the sky. The project, for downtown Miami, would have included over two and a half million square feet of mixed-use space.

→ CAMPUS CENTER WRITHES SKYWARD TOWARD ITS COMMANDING CROWN.

← THE LOWER PUBLIC SPACES, FORMED BY THE ANGLED MASSING OF
THE BUILDING, FRAME ONE OF MIAMI'S BEST-KNOWN LANDMARKS,
LIBERTY TOWER.

GUY W. PETERSON, NCARB, FAIA

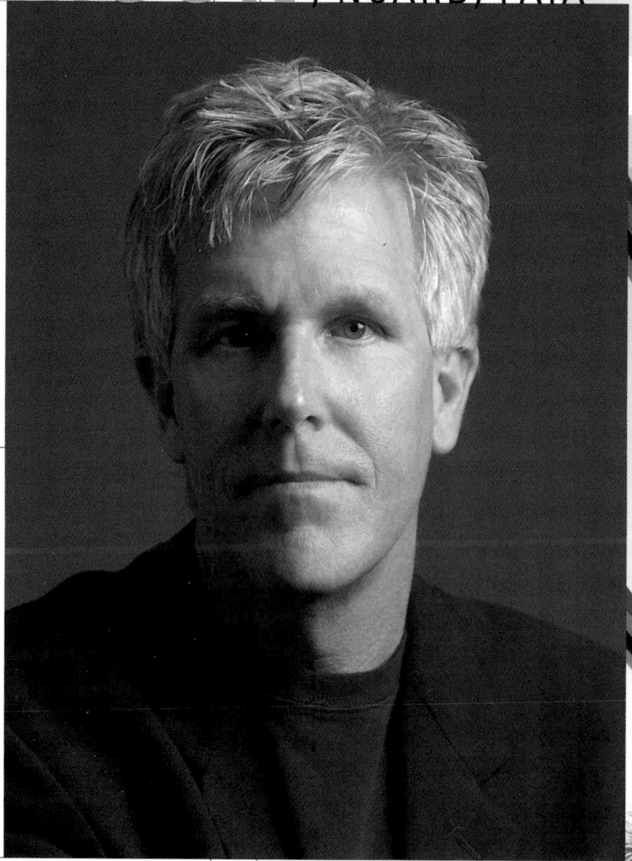

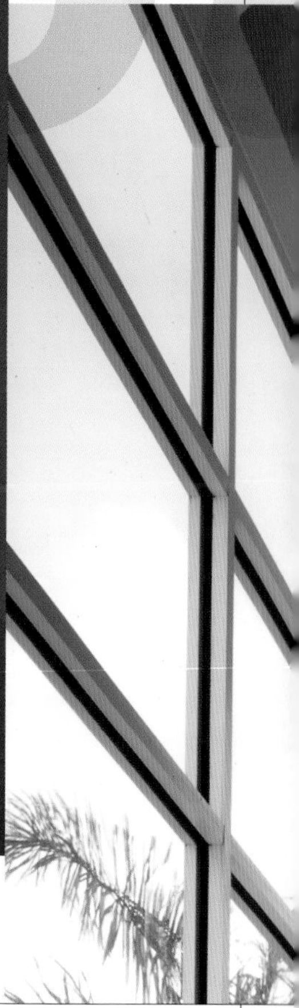

Guy Peterson | Office for Architecture | Sarasota, Florida

During an interview with Peter Blake, Paul Rudolph stated, "Structure seldom humanizes, but appropriate space always touches humans."[1] Given his lifelong proximity to the lauded projects of the Sarasota School giants, first among them Paul Rudolph, it's natural that Guy Peterson aims to infuse the spaces he designs with the experiential.

Having been surrounded by the Sarasota School aesthetic during his impressionable years, it is equally natural that he would take up the cause and carry the vernacular into the future.

"I went to elementary school in a Victor Lundy building, to junior high school in a Ralph and William Zimmerman building, and to Rudolph's Riverview High School," says Peterson, who was eight months old when his parents moved the family to Sarasota. "My dad, who was a doctor, practiced in a Zimmerman building; I swam at Ralph Twitchell's Lido Casino and went to the Field Club, which Tim Seibert designed—I was literally steeped in the Sarasota School aesthetic!"

Even with this bombardment of unconscious stimuli, it wasn't until he was in high school that Peterson con- sciously realized the power of architecture. "I answered an ad in the paper to help clear away the property of a house on Siesta Key after a tropical storm had blown through the area," he explains. "I'd never seen a house like the one that commanded that property before: it was all exposed block, walls of glass, black frames, and beautiful modern art. I later learned that Gene Leedy had designed the house for the artist Syd Solomon."

In graduate school at the University of Florida, Peterson chose the graduate design program, which was overseen by Harry Merritt. "Harry was a Harvard graduate who had studied under Walter Gropius and Bucky Fuller," Peterson says. "He was a talented architect who understood Le Corbusier, Gropius, and the Bauhaus—influences that he naturally passed on through the curriculum."

Producing significant public projects in Tallahassee and Sarasota was Peterson's focus early in his career. It wasn't until he was designing a home for his parents in Sarasota that a strong realization came over him: he recognized an intense yearning to concentrate his efforts on residential work. Armed with his favorite caveat, "When you get it right, you have nothing to remove," he has since created an extensive body of work based on minimalist principles. He refers to the level of minimalism that he achieves as essentialism. "I design by reduction, not by addition; by analysis, not by comparison," he says. "I like to look at projects and keep pulling things back until all that's left is beautiful space and light."

John Howey, FAIA, an architect and author who has written extensively about Florida architecture, says of Guy, "Rare is the architect who grew up experiencing authentic architecture, in this case 1950s Sarasota modern; who saw the range of architectural directions in the 1980s; and who returned to create a meaningful architecture that expressed the essence of Florida's subtropical climate and its building traditions. Guy Peterson exemplifies this with his distinct sense of volume, light and shade."[2] Using these tools of his trade, Peterson strives to create spaces that provide the unfolding of experience. "Maybe the experiences won't be cognitive for everyone who walks through one of the buildings I've designed," he explains, "but I always want there to be a feeling of enjoyment."

→ THE THEISEN RESIDENCE ILLUSTRATES THE DRAMA PETERSON ACHIEVES WITH HIS ARCHITECTURE.

ANALYSIS **by Warren R. Schwartz, FAIA, principal of Boston-based Schwartz/Silver Architects**

With the simplest of means, Guy Peterson has pursued and developed a rich architectural vision based on the legacy of the Sarasota School.

I became aware of Peterson's work when I had the opportunity to meet him and visit some of his extraordinary houses. As a native Floridian myself, I was aware of the struggle to create meaningful architecture expressing the essential characteristics of Florida's subtropical climate and building traditions. Two generations ago, the original and optimistic Gulf Coast houses of Paul Rudolph succeeded.

But recent "revival" architecture eroded that blend of indigenous and modern architecture.

The work of Guy Peterson has begun to reestablish this authentic regional aesthetic and to redefine and extend the range of the Sarasota School. He begins with the basics of climate, program, volume, and proportion, and creates buildings of simplicity and power that are both conceptually direct and spatially complex.

Although quite different in program, siting, and circumstance, Peterson's buildings spring from the sense that architecture is made from simple materials carefully employed to accommodate function, sculpt space, and capture light. With clarity of form, he combines the fundamental elements of construction to define spaces with surprising variety, so much so that one searches out every space to experience its "feel." Finally, one stands back and "reads" the proportions, lines, surfaces, openings, light and shadow that give the buildings their individual character.

Throughout the past decade Guy Peterson has explored and layered in deliberative fashion qualities of wall, color, cadence, suspension, texture, and context to achieve an architecture rich in form, at once familiar but recognizable as his own. Peterson seems to have begun by staking out the boundaries of his own architectural inquiry in the designs of the Theisen Residence (1997) and the Freund Residence (2000). The first is a study in white surfaces and linear space, while the second utilizes color, column grid, and free plan. The sensibility of the first is brilliant clarity, monumentality, and expansiveness; the second is full of shadowed complexity, impromptu spaces, and introspection. The differences

← PETERSON'S ANACLERIO RESIDENCE IS DEEPLY FRAMED AND SHADOWED AGAINST A GROVE OF ROYAL PALMS.

↑ BRILLIANT CLARITY, MONUMENTALITY, AND EXPANSIVENESS CHARACTERIZE PETERSON'S THEISEN RESIDENCE.

may have had more to do with the clients than the architecture, but these two houses serve to provide the frame of reference for what followed.

The romance of sky, water, beach grass, and palm bring Peterson's architectural vocabulary into a more natural landscape in the Anaclerio Residence (2003) and the House on Bird Key (2004). Although primarily white, the first is spatially complex, rhythmic in its balance of interior spaces against a grove of royal palms—deeply framed, shadowed. Similarly, the second is framed, folded, and suspended. Both meet the requirement of houses to be elevated above flood tide. The piano nobile contributes to the distinctive form of Florida's coastal architecture and Rudolph's Sarasota School buildings.

Finally and most recently, Guy Peterson has redefined the neighborhood house, on Hawthorne Street (2005), and offered his own example of restoration and new addition (2007) to the Revere Quality House (1948) by Paul Rudolph and Ralph Twitchell. Both the Hawthorne Street House and the original Revere Quality House are modest one-story houses. The house on Hawthorne Street is rooted in modern Florida architecture of the 1940s through 1960s, and it is built of readily available materials. This house gains its beauty through simplicity, proportion, and asymmetry, and

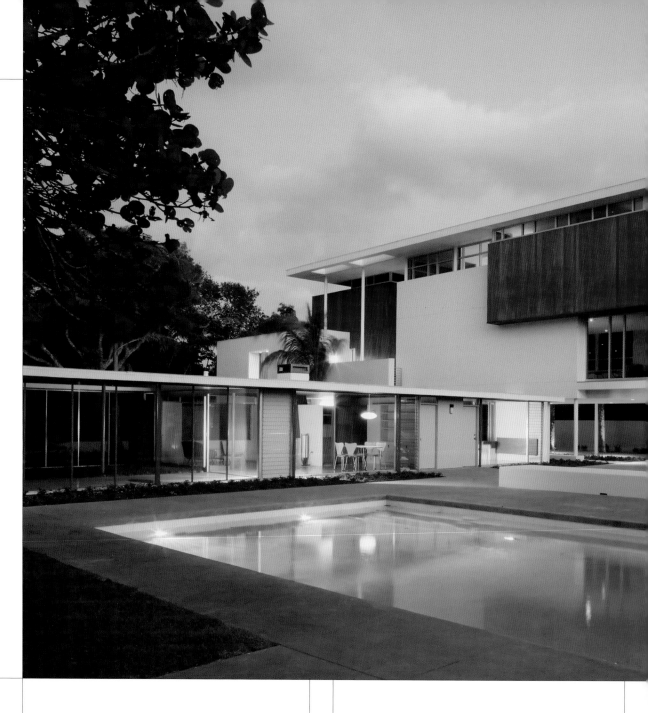

its livability through materials, textures, and furnishings. Whereas the use of color at Hawthorne Street is limited to its materials palette, color drifts through the Revere Quality House and its new three-story addition.

Each house we've considered contains a pool within or just outside the structure itself, but the Hawthorne Street House places the pool in the center of the L-shaped composition. At the Revere Quality House the pool is placed at the far end of the original house and reflects the full addition in its surface. This house could be seen as a culmination of Peterson's explorations to date (studies of the qualities of wall, color, cadence, suspension, texture, and context) but it goes beyond and charts a new course for his architecture.

It is as if the original Revere Quality House has become Adam's rib to the new building. Materials that were heretofore inside are now outside as well, providing scale, texture, and the color of wood to the mostly white exterior surfaces. Although glass defines the interior spaces, overhangs, floor projections, and soffits define the outdoor spaces and blur the distinction between inside and out. Color is used on steel columns and on ceilings as well as on walls. The trees on the site, many of them three stories tall, are echoed by the new structure. The overall composition is as effortless as the original. The new and old are both renewed.

Guy Peterson's houses will be placed among our current best, not only within the context of regional architecture, but within American architecture in general. They succeed in extending the range of the Sarasota School and the influence of modern architecture into the twenty-first century.

← SCHWARTZ REMARKS THAT THE ORIGINAL REVERE QUALITY HOUSE BECOMES "ADAM'S RIB" TO PETERSON'S NEW BUILDING.

Saxon Henry: Who would you describe as influences in your work?

As I've grown as an architect over the years, I have gone through periods during which I've shed certain things and moved on, but I have always seen my work as a blend of the Sarasota School and other influences, both from my life and from things I've studied. Though my work certainly falls under the category of a Florida regional modernism, there are other modernist attitudes in other regions of the world that have similar climates, like Mexico, from which I draw inspiration.

I've grown to appreciate how light is handled by architects other than just the Sarasota School. Take Louis Barragán, for example. I've been a huge fan of his work since I discovered it in 1980. I enjoy the simplicity of his designs, and how he approaches volumes and cubes. The way the New York Five, Gwathmey and Meier in particular, handled structure and used it to define space was a major influence, and of course, Le Corbusier.

With the architects I admire, I attempt to break down how they approach their projects. Take Rudolph, for example: to a great extent, he was building a tropical interpretation of International Style principles in Sarasota. On the other hand, Victor Lundy, who was also a Sarasota School architect, had a much more emotional approach to movement in his work. It wasn't as rigid and defined by the International Style—it was almost Corbusier out of wood.

The component of my work that has the International Style rationalism, logic, proportion, rhythm, balance, expres-

sionist structure, and free plan is a Miesian attitude. Then there's the passionate, emotional part of what I do that's Corb in the sense that I'm not just dealing with columns and beams but with volumes, masses, and voids. In this sense, those voids become vessels that the light moves through and space is defined through that. That's what Barragán would do in his work and it's why I admire it.

Why do you think that architects like Mies and Le Corbusier, who were being studied at Harvard during Rudolph's time, have had such an effect on your design philosophies?

I think there's a unique beauty in each of their approaches and attitudes about architecture, and they've influenced me differently, so I would say my work is more a synthesis of those ideas rather than representative of either one in particular. They certainly were the giants of the day, but they are not the only ones. Look at Wright: I don't think there's an architect living who wasn't influenced by Frank Lloyd Wright in terms of scale, proportion, geometry, and movement through space.

Geometry is an important element in my work. I love to work off of grid and use that grid as a constant defining element, but only to the point that it makes sense. In other words, it's essential not to force the design but to work it to the point that it has logic behind it. Wright was great at that.

Another thing that I think is very important in my work, which is more noticeable in my current work, is minimalism. Ten years ago or so, I began thinking about a minimalist ap-

→ THE BIRD KEY HOUSE IS AN EXPRESSION OF DYNAMICALLY FRAMED, FOLDED, AND SUSPENDED FORMS.

proach with a greater simplicity and honesty to it. I like to create a space and then take things away from it so that I'm left with just the pure form. There are architects, like John Pawson in England, who do this so well. I think he's one of the superior minds in minimalism when it comes to architecture.

Claudio Silvestrin and Alberto Campo Baeza also have similar attitudes of simplifying, which means they end up with these spaces and forms that are defined by light. They create spaces that are devoid of ornament and the detail is in the minimalist nature of them—the way the floor meets the wall or the way the ceiling floats out into space with glass that slices through it. Spaces with these attributes look as if they would be easier to create, but they are in fact more difficult.

Why is that?

When there are fewer layers, architects have to be more analytical about how they are designing, because fewer things are covered over. Detailing is really important in our work, but it's not just about the space and the form that we are creating; at the end of the day it's about standing in the space—touching it and seeing it up close. At that point, designing is like hitting the head of a pin: it only works if we get it right.

Would you say that your creative process slowly simmers, or do you normally have an immediate "Aha!" when designing a project?

There are eureka moments, but I usually let things simmer for quite a while, though I'm not always conscious of the fact that I'm thinking about projects. I swim every day and I'm in the water for forty-five minutes. I will sometimes have inspired ideas come to me when I'm swimming. This is likely the result of the fact that no one is talking to me, the phone is not ringing, and bubbles are all I hear. I also think it's because I'm relaxed and my mind is relaxed.

If I'm working on something and I'm trying to develop a concept, before the solution occurs to me there has been quite a bit of unconscious preparation. Once I gather all of the information on a project, it goes into the blender. I consider the owner's program—for instance, what they don't like is more important to me than what they do like; the site and the different issues related to the context in which they are building; and if a project is on the water, the slew of jurisdictional and coastal requirements that we have to deal with.

I don't begin a project by merely looking at the property; I start with the approach to the site. The first thing I usually do is to ask myself how I am going to physically approach the site. When someone drives up, how are they going to enter the property? My design process begins with this coming toward the site. Once I understand the site and how someone will be entering it, I begin working with a diagram of the site to see how the house will interplay with the site influences. Maybe in my mind I'm already blocking out programmatic functions, but I'm concentrating on the physical aspects of the site.

Do you draw these early approaches or do you use a computer?

Everything I design is with a pencil and tracing paper. I don't design a plan and then try to extrude it to see how it looks.

I will often have the full three-dimensional elevations to the house completely drawn in presentation quality before I finalize the plans. This is important, because by that time I know where the spaces are as I've been slowly shaping the building. In this respect, I do the three-dimensional part of the planning process way before it's time to do the finalized, drawn plans.

I think there's something very intuitive about drawing— even the sound of the pencil rasping across the paper is stimulating. With a pencil, you can make a little curve and start working with that, but if you're on a computer, your eyes are looking at a screen and you're moving your mouse while seeing something move. This feels restrictive to me.

Maybe I'm dating myself, but I do a presentation of pencil drawings, and it's not until the client approves them that we take them to CAD and create the 3-D models.

Having said that, the computer has opened up worlds that were impossible before the technology was available to us, as it allows us to create forms that had never been created before. Bilbao is a great example of this. A computer is also an important production and marketing tool. For instance, there is a Richard Meier project that I saw in a magazine on an airplane the other day, and I couldn't tell

↓ THESE HAND-DRAWN ELEVATIONS OF THE FREUND RESIDENCE ILLUSTRATE THE LEVEL OF DETAIL PETERSON ACHIEVES BEFORE HIS DESIGN TEAM TURNS TO THE COMPUTER TO CREATE DIGITAL 3-D MODELS.

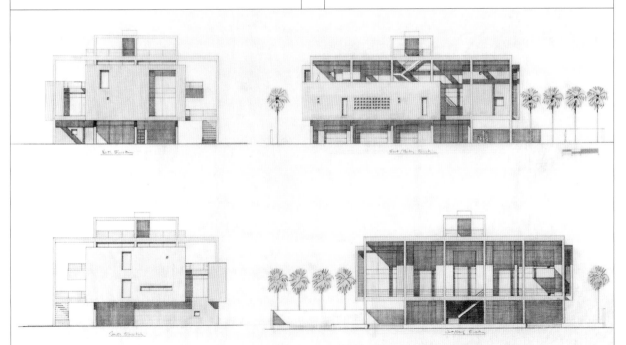

if it was a real building or a computer rendering. Still, they are just going to have to bury me with a pencil, a scale, and a roll of tracing paper!

Do you travel, and, if so, does traveling inform your work?

Italy is one of my favorite countries. I had the opportunity to spend three weeks there with a number of architects from around the world in 1996. From an architectural point of view, that was a high point in my life. I had the opportunity to meet Aldo Rossi and Mario Botta. We went to Turin to Renzo Piano's Fiat factory, to Lake Como to see Giuseppe Terragni's early work, to Lugano in Switzerland to see Botta's work. Then we went to Vicenza and to Verona to see Carlo Scarpa's Castelvecchio Museum and Palladio's work. We also visited Venice, Padua, Pisa, Rome, and Florence. We were allowed to go into the most incredible buildings and meet some of the architects who designed them.

My wife and I have also traveled throughout France, and I try to go on at least one architectural odyssey in this country every year. I'll go to Santa Monica, Chicago, Arizona, Minneapolis, or New York—wherever I can see in person the projects that I have seen published, or can see the work of the architects whom I admire.

When you return from trips, do you see an immediate impact on your work?

I don't necessarily think the work that I see relates to what I'm doing, but it reaffirms my dedication to quality and renews my determination to be true to my profession. In other words, when I travel and I see significant architecture first-hand, it refocuses my energy toward my commitment to do it right. That's the thing I gain the most.

In terms of the physical, I do see approaches to space, to detailing, and to the way other architects resolve different things—like the way they capture light, which I'll sketch into notebooks. Perhaps the next time I start a project, I'll remember how someone else executed a particular element and see if some of those concepts would apply to interpreting it my way. It may be intangible and a little harder to measure, but I do pick up new attitudes and a renewed passion for what I do when I travel.

I also find traveling to be a very important part of my education as an architect. The only way I can keep my work from becoming stale or stagnant is through traveling and through journals. These are my connections to the architectural world.

You talk about creating experiences with your work. What do you mean by that?

To a great extent, I believe that architecture is about progression and sequence through space. I consider this from the very beginning when I design the experience of arriving. When someone approaches the entrance to one of my projects, I don't necessarily want to give everything away at the start. I want people to know where they should go, but I don't want them to know how to enter the building immediately. I want even this to be gleaned through a process of discovery.

Once they are at the point of entering the structure, I want the experience to be an unfolding one. I don't want to have someone throw the door open to a house on the Gulf

→ PETERSON'S INTENTION WAS TO CREATE ETHEREAL LAYERS OF MINIMALISM WITHIN THE THEISEN RESIDENCE, AS THIS VIEW FROM THE MAIN HOUSE TOWARD THE GUESTHOUSE SHOWS.

→ EXPERIENTIAL MOVEMENT THROUGH THE SPACES HE DESIGNS IS A HALLMARK OF PETERSON'S ARCHITECTURE.

of Mexico, for example, and immediately see the view. I'd rather have someone enter and see a painting, a plane, or a surface. It's not a halting element, but something that makes them want to go around the corner that is just at the edge of their vision. I like for my buildings to offer a series of smaller epiphanies, even if there is a big impression at the end of the journey.

My work is really about suspense, which means continuing surprises and relationships with circulation that create tension. I try to set up relationships within my spaces so that as you move through them, they have meaning. It's not just about the big gulf view; there are garden views and internal views—spaces between structures. Often, I'll break a house down into different buildings, and one building may not be attached to the other. It's that space between the buildings that becomes as important as the space within the buildings. I like to think that my architecture taps into the curiosity of those who are traversing through it. It's a similar notion to when I'm walking down a narrow European street in a quaint town: I see a building that sits at a bit of an angle and it draws me to it. Let's say that the building is angling to the right. I go down the long alley and as I approach, it influences me to go right. That's how architecture can participate in the experience we have of places.

SARASOTA MEMORIAL HOSPITAL
CRITICAL CARE CENTER, 1993

Sarasota, Florida

The Critical Care Center was a joint venture between Guy Peterson | Office for Architecture and Nix Mann and Associates of Atlanta—a prominent firm specializing in healthcare projects, which was responsible for the medical planning and the building's interiors. The design process spanned five years and was Peterson's last significant public project. The restrictive size of the property led him to design a sculptural building that takes advantage of light and views deep into the structure. This project garnered his firm awards from the Georgia and the Florida Gulf Coast chapters of the AIA.

↓ THE MASSING OF THE BUILDING FLOATS ON PILOTIS ABOVE THE EMERGENCY ROOM, WHICH TAKES UP THE ENTIRE GROUND LEVEL.

→ THE PROTRUDING RECTANGLE ABOVE THE ENTRANCE TO EMERGENCY SERVICES HOLDS THE SECOND-FLOOR SURGICAL WAITING ROOMS.

PROJECTS

↓ COLUMNS SUPPORT A NUMBER OF EXTERIOR PAVILIONS. THE PILOTIS FRAME OPEN VOIDS WITHIN THE STRUCTURE, CREATING THE ILLUSION THAT THE PAVILIONS ARE SCULPTED FROM THE BUILDING'S MASSING.

← ONE OF THREE SURGERY "PODS" JUTS OUT FROM THE STRUCTURE.

↓ CUBES EXTENDING BEYOND THE BUILDING'S FACADE AND ABOVE A DATUM DELINEATING THE BREAK BETWEEN FLOORS CREATE THAT INTERPLAY OF SOLIDS AND VOIDS THAT GIVE PETERSON'S ARCHITECTURE A POWERFUL GEOMETRIC QUALITY.

THEISEN RESIDENCE, 1997

Bradenton, Florida

The main consideration for the design of this residence was unobstructed views toward Sarasota Bay. The 10,000-square-foot home recedes in scale as it progresses from the front volumetric to the guesthouse in the back. By angling the forwardmost protruding element, in which Peterson placed covered outdoor spaces, to forty-five degrees, he opened the views to the north. Both the Florida Association of the AIA and the Gulf Coast Chapter gave the firm an Award of Excellence for this home.

↓ SITE PLAN.

→ THE FRONT CUBE, WITH ITS CURTAIN WALLS OF UNBRAISED GLASS, THREE STORIES HIGH ON THE BAY-FACING FACADE, CONTAINS THE MAIN LIVING AREAS.

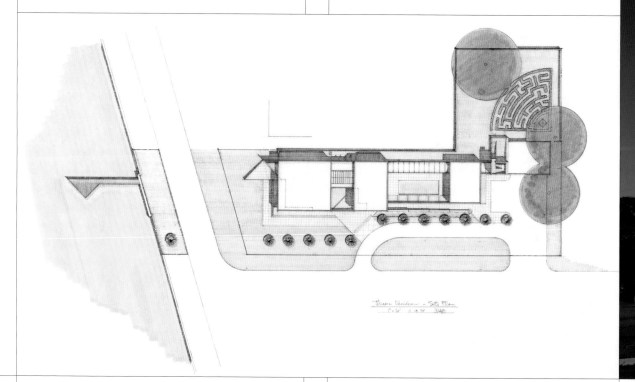

↑ A VIEW FROM THE GUEST LIVING ROOM TOWARD THE MAIN HOUSE
SHOWS THE HOME'S INTERMINGLING OF TRANSPARENCY AND OPAQUENESS, AS
IN THE PROTRUDING OPAQUE BOX FILLED WITH CURTAIN WALLS AND
BALCONIES.

↑ BOTH LARGE AND SMALL DETAILS ABOUND, FROM VAULTED ROOFS
TO SMALL PERFORATIONS ON THE COURTYARD WALL THAT ALLOW AIR TO FILTER
IN.

↑ WITH ITS SERIES OF VOLUMES AND FORMS, THE INTERIOR SPACES OF THE RESIDENCE ARE DYNAMIC RATHER THAN STATIC, ENCOURAGING MOVEMENT WHILE MAINTAINING A SCALE THAT IS NOT OVERWHELMING.

↑ IN THE OWNER'S PRIVATE LIVING ROOM, THE ABUNDANCE OF NATURAL LIGHT IS EBULLIENT.

↑ THOUGH MONOCHROMATIC, THE INTERIOR COLOR SCHEME IS FAR FROM SIMPLE, WITH NINE DIFFERENT SHADES OF WHITE, SHOWN HERE IN THE LIVING ROOM.

THE REVERE QUALITY HOUSE, 2007

Sarasota, Florida

The Revere Quality House presented Peterson with the opportunity to renovate and design an addition to a Paul Rudolph/Ralph Twitchell building. "It was emotional," he recalls. "I tried to think about how Rudolph would reinterpret the project." The original house, the low-slung one-story building, was in dire shape when Peterson's client bought the property. Because of his respect for Rudolph's work, the architect convinced the homeowner to restore the original building and to gain the additional space he desired with a new addition. The Florida AIA recognized Peterson's firm with an Unbuilt Award and the Gulf Coast Chapter a Merit Award for this renovation and addition.

→ THE IPÉ-CLAD VOLUMES THAT PROTRUDE FROM THE EXTERIOR OF THE NEW BUILDING REFLECT STRIATED PLYWOOD ELEMENTS CONTAINED WITHIN IN THE ORIGINAL HOUSE, NOW A GUESTHOUSE.

↑ THE WINDOW GRID SYSTEM WAS DESIGNED TO ACHIEVE A RHYTHM THAT FEELS SIMILAR TO THE SCREENED FRONT OF THE ORIGINAL STRUCTURE.

→ MANY OF THE INTERIOR ELEMENTS HAD TO BE REFURBISHED OR RE-CREATED, SUCH AS THE TERRAZZO FLOORS AND THE JALOUSIE WINDOWS AND BLINDS.

1 carport
2 courtyard
3 living
4 dining
5 kitchen
6 bedroom
7 pool & terrace
8 dock
9 parking court
10 garage
11 entry
12 entry foyer
13 outdoor living

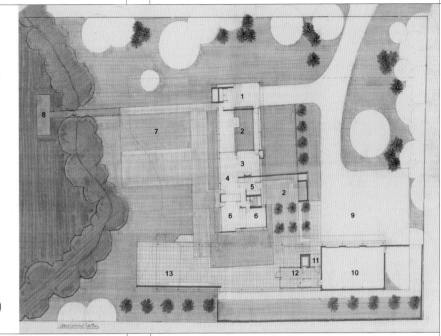

N

↑ SITE PLAN.

← MATERIALS USED IN THE INTERIORS OF THE NEW RESIDENCE, SUCH AS THE WOOD ELEMENTS SEEN HERE, ARE REFLECTIVE OF THE MATERIALS IN THE ORIGINAL BUILDING.

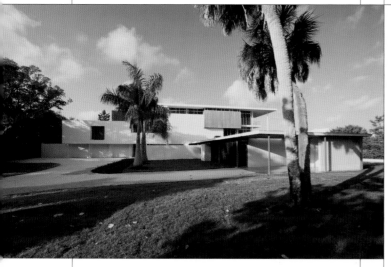

↑ PETERSON WAS CAREFUL TO ENSURE THAT
THE PRESENCE OF THE NEW BUILDING WAS NOT
FELT FROM WITHIN THE INTERIORS OF THE
ORIGINAL BUILDING.

→ A LOW WALL THAT EXTENDED FROM THE
ORIGINAL HOUSE NOW FORMS THE BOUNDARY
OF A COURTYARD THAT CONNECTS THE
TWO BUILDINGS.

← THE TRANSPARENCY OF THE ORIGINAL BUILDING COMBINES WITH THE LAYERING OF VOLUMES AND FORMS OF THE NEW BUILDING TO CREATE A COMPLEX BUT SEAMLESS RELATIONSHIP BETWEEN THE TWO STRUCTURES.

↓ ORIGINAL DRAWINGS AND ELEVATIONS BY RUDOLPH AND TWITCHELL.

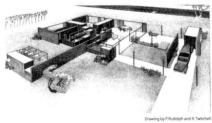

Drawing by P. Rudolph and R. Twitchell

Drawing by P. Rudolph and R. Twitchell

Drawing by P. Rudolph and R. Twitchell

MORRIS RESIDENCE, 1998

Sarasota, Florida

This residence on Casey Key rose from the footprint of a nondescript one-story dwelling, whose existence allowed a closer proximity to the water but hindered the size and height of the home. Within the interiors, interlocking volumes weave together to form a progression through the home's varied spaces. An entry sequence progresses through telescoping bamboo and minimal architecture, culminating in a courtyard with Turkish pots and a carved geometric form filled with water.

→ THE MASTER BEDROOM SUITE IS SITUATED ON THE SECOND FLOOR, AND THE MIDDLE PAVILION IS THE LIVING ROOM; THE TWO ARE CONNECTED BY A GLASS ATRIUM STAIRWELL. THE SMALLEST CUBE HOLDS THE GUEST BEDROOM.

← THIS VIEW OF THE STRUCTURE SHOWS HOW IMPORTANT THE MASSING IS AS IT FOLDS INTO DIFFERENT VOLUMES AND FORMS IN A PROGRESSION THROUGH THE COURTYARD.

↓ THE BAMBOO IS A NATURAL SCULPTURE SET IN CONCRETE — ONE OF MANY EXPERIENCES IN THE ENTRY SEQUENCE.

→ THE VESSEL SPOUTING WATER BRINGS THE SENSUALITY OF SUBTLE SPLASHING SOUNDS TO THE COURTYARD.

← THE LIGHT POURING INTO THE INTERIORS PROVES WHAT A POWERFUL ELEMENT NATURAL ILLUMINATION CAN BE WHEN ARCHITECTURE IS DESIGNED TO INTERACT WITH IT.

↑ THE STAIRWAY IS OPEN TO THE GULF, CREATING ONE OF THE KEY MOMENTS PETERSON SEEKS WHEN HE'S DESIGNING ARCHITECTURE. STEEL SPACERS IN THE WALL SUPPORT THE HORIZONTAL TREADS ON ONE SIDE, WHILE AN OFFSET STRINGER LEAVES THE VIEW OF A PERSON ASCENDING THE STAIRS UNHINDERED.

BETAGOLE RESIDENCE, 1999

Longboat Key, Florida

Though Peterson's client wanted a modern design, the restrictions within this neighborhood required a pitched roof. The architect accomplished both by designing an entry pavilion that reads as a statuesque glass gallery. A rounded roof detail recalls Le Corbusier's design of the Villa Savoye. Shell concrete, pale wood, and white surfaces bring an elemental feel to the interiors. To reflect the home's triangular footprint, Peterson punctured the overhang facing the gulf with triangular perforations.

→ A COURTYARD WALL LEADING TO THE ENTRY REPEATS THE SHAPE OF THE WATER ELEMENT AS IT TAPERS OFF, A SUBTLE EXAMPLE OF PETERSON'S RIGOR.

← THE PATTERNING OF THE FRAMEWORK FOR TWO SCREENED PORCHES, WHICH FLANK A WALL OF GLASS, ECHO THE WINDOW GRID. THE PUNCTURES IN THE ROOF OVERHANG ALLOW SUNLIGHT TO WAFT INTO THE COMMANDING LOGGIA.

↑ THE ROUNDED SHAPE THAT PROTRUDES ABOVE THE ROOF IS THE TOP OF A SIXTEEN-FOOT-TALL CYLINDRICAL SHOWER.

↑ THE FREE PLAN IS EXPRESSED IN THIS RESIDENCE WITH COLUMNS THAT RISE INDEPENDENT OF THE OUTER ENVELOPE OF THE STRUCTURE.

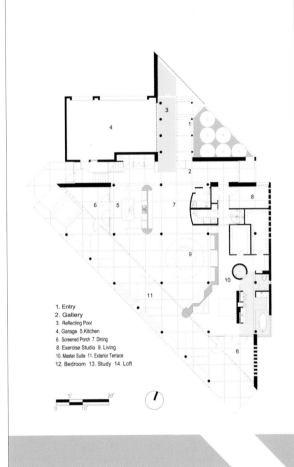

1. Entry
2. Gallery
3. Reflecting Pool
4. Garage 5.Kitchen
6. Screened Porch 7. Dining
8. Exercise Studio 9. Living
10. Master Suite 11. Exterior Terrace
12. Bedroom 13. Study 14. Loft

← AN INTERIOR POOL, WITH ITS MASSIVE COLUMNS THAT MARCH ALONG A WALL INSET WITH GLASS BLOCK, FORMS A DRAMATIC ELEMENT.

↑ THE STATUESQUE GLASS GALLERY IS FLANKED BY THE MAIN ENTRY ON THE LEFT AND THE ENTRANCE TO THE MASTER BEDROOM ON THE RIGHT.

→ FLOOR PLAN.

FREUND RESIDENCE, 2000

Siesta Key, Florida

The owners of this 7,652-square-foot residence asked Peterson for dynamic colorful elements, which he introduced in different cubes that represent varying activities—purple for the main living space; white for the shared areas of dining, exercise, and library; yellow for the private master bedroom suite; and orange for the children's quarters. He took cues from Le Corbusier's free plan to develop the home's series of volumetric forms that float within a concrete frame. The Freund Residence earned Peterson's firm an Honor Award from the Florida Gulf Coast Chapter of the AIA and an Excellence in Architecture Award from the Florida Association of the AIA.

→ THE NATURAL SIMPLICITY AND RHYTHM OF THE STRADDLING CONCRETE FRAME IS AUSTERE IN ITS HUMBLE MATERIALS BUT COMPLEX IN ITS RELATIONSHIP TO THE STRUCTURE AND ITS DETAILED WINDOW WALLS.

↑ THE COLORS OF THE DIFFERENT VOLUMES ARE THOSE OF THE SEASHELLS FOUND AROUND SIESTA KEY.

→ PETERSON PULLED THE CONCRETE ROOF AWAY FROM THE OUTER FRAME SO THAT THE FACADE WOULD BE WASHED WITH SUNLIGHT.

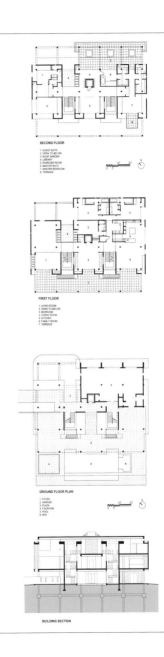

SECOND FLOOR

1. GUEST SUITE
2. OPEN TO BELOW
3. ROOF GARDEN
4. LIBRARY
5. EXERCISE ROOM
6. MASTER BATH
7. MASTER BEDROOM
8. TERRACE

FIRST FLOOR

1. LIVING ROOM
2. OPEN TO BELOW
3. BEDROOM
4. DINING ROOM
5. KITCHEN
6. FAMILY ROOM
7. TERRACE

GROUND FLOOR PLAN

1. FOYER
2. GARAGE
3. PLAZA
4. FOUNTAIN
5. POOL
6. SPA

BUILDING SECTION

← IN THE VIEW TOWARD THE FORMAL LIVING ROOM IT IS CLEAR THAT THIS PROJECT IS MORE "MUSCULAR" THAN MANY OF PETERSON'S DESIGNS.

↑ THE DRAMATIC CURTAIN WALL OF THE THREE-STORY FOYER WAS MADE POSSIBLE BY THE TWELVE-INCH CONCRETE COLUMNS THAT SUPPORT PETERSON'S FREE PLAN.

→ GROUND, FIRST-FLOOR, AND SECOND-FLOOR PLANS, AS WELL AS BUILDING SECTION (BOTTOM).

WILLIAMS RESIDENCE, 2001

Sarasota, Florida

The site holding this winter home steps down to the water on a narrow piece of property. The exterior spaces were as important to the homeowners as the interior spaces, so the outdoor "rooms" that are not open to the water are carved out of partially protected courtyard and terrace spaces. The owners, an Oregon couple, asked Peterson to include wood in his design schematic to satisfy their fondness for the warmth the material brings to a home's aesthetics. This project won Merit Awards from the Gulf Coast Chapter and the Florida Association of the AIA, and an Award of Excellence in Architecture from the Florida Association.

→ CREATING A STRONG SYMMETRY, AN OPAQUE CUBE FITTED WITH A CYCLOPSIAN SHADOW-BOX WINDOW BALANCES WITH A WALL THAT THRUSTS ABOVE TWO VARYING ROOFLINES ON THE OPPOSITE SIDE OF THE STRUCTURE.

↑↑ THE DRAMATIC LIVING ROOM IS WRAPPED ON THREE SIDES BY WALLS OF WOOD-FRAMED WINDOWS.

↑ A SECOND-STORY GARDEN, PROTECTED BY A JUTTING OVERHANG, INTERSECTS AN ADJOINING BALCONY THAT SPANS THE ENTRY TO THE TERRACE, ONE OF THE INDEPENDENT ELEMENTS THAT CONSISTENTLY INFORM PETERSON'S ARCHITECTURE.

→ A WALL, WHICH SUPPORTS A BALCONY WITH A STRIATED DETAIL, DISSECTS TWIN WALKWAYS LEADING TO THE TERRACE AREA AND THE FRONT ENTRY—AN EXAMPLE OF THE CARE PETERSON TAKES WHEN CREATING PROGRESSIONS TOWARD HIS BUILDINGS.

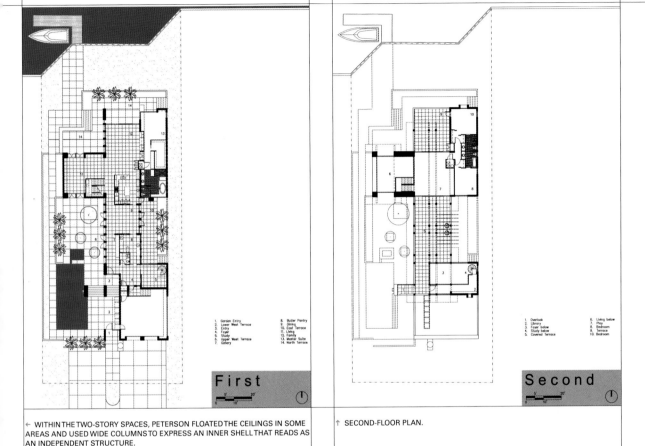

1. Garden Entry
2. Lower West Terrace
3. Entry
4. Foyer
5. Study
6. Upper West Terrace
7. Gallery
8. Butler Pantry
9. Dining
10. East Terrace
11. Living
12. Family
13. Master Suite
14. North Terrace

First

1. Overlook
2. Library
3. Foyer below
4. Study below
5. Covered Terrace
6. Living below
7. Play
8. Bedroom
9. Terrace
10. Bedroom

Second

← WITHIN THE TWO-STORY SPACES, PETERSON FLOATED THE CEILINGS IN SOME AREAS AND USED WIDE COLUMNS TO EXPRESS AN INNER SHELL THAT READS AS AN INDEPENDENT STRUCTURE.

↑ FIRST-FLOOR PLAN.

↑ SECOND-FLOOR PLAN.

LONGBOAT KEY POLICE STATION, 2001

Longboat Key, Florida

Peterson refers to this simple 6,500-square-foot building with a mono-pitch roof as a sort of Rubik's cube of shapes. The sloping shed roof and unassuming architecture are indicative of the resoluteness of the building's activities, but the forms that wriggle under the sloping roof are expressive. Peterson describes the building as having a quiet presence on the island.

→ ABSTRACTLY BALANCED WINDOW FENESTRATIONS ARE DARK ELEMENTS DURING DAYLIGHT HOURS; THE PROTRUDING WALL THAT SHOOTS UP THROUGH THE ROOF PLANE FROM THE ARMORY PROVIDES A CONTRASTING LIGHT ELEMENT.

← A SHADOW-BOX WINDOW PROJECTING OUT FROM THE SQUAD ROOM SEEMS TO SERVE AS A COUNTERBALANCE TO THE RISING ROOFLINE.

↑ PETERSON'S DETAILS ARE OFTEN SUBTLE, SUCH AS THE SHAPE OF THESE LIGHTING ELEMENTS THAT REPEAT THE ANGULAR PROFILE OF THE BUILDING.

→ A WALL TELESCOPES OUT AND ANGLES OFF, MIMICKING THE SLOPE OF THE ROOF—A SUBTLE BUT DEMONSTRATIVE DETAIL.

ANACLERIO RESIDENCE, 2003

Longboat Key, Florida

This beach house on the Gulf of Mexico had to be compact because of the narrowness of the parcel. Coastal restrictions forced Peterson to site the home at the eastern edge of the property, which places it close to the street. Its simple street-side composition was designed for privacy, while the free plan on the gulf-facing facade opens the interiors to water views. The floating exterior loft, formed by an extended upper roofline, serves as sun and wind protection without interfering with the panoramic vistas. The Florida Association of the AIA recognized this project with an Unbuilt Award and an Award of Excellence in Architecture.

→ THE FREE PLAN ALLOWED PETERSON TO SCULPT THE SPACE OF THIS RESIDENCE AROUND ITS STRUCTURE TO ACHIEVE A DYNAMIC AND HONEST RESULT.

← THE HOUSE FLOATS ABOVE THE POOL AND SPA AREA. A TRELLIS-LIKE
GRATE CARVED INTO THE OVERHANG CREATES AN OPPORTUNITY FOR THE
ARCHITECTURE TO INTERACT WITH LIGHT.

→ RATHER THAN EXTENDING THE STRUCTURE OF THE HOUSE TO CREATE AN
OVERHANG FOR THE POOL AND BALCONY, PETERSON DESIGNED A CONCRETE
FRAME THAT BECOMES AN EXPRESSIVE INDEPENDENT ELEMENT. IT IS THIS
LEVEL OF DETAILING THAT MAKES PETERSON'S ARCHITECTURE VISUALLY RICH.

↑ THE STREET-FACING FACADE, RAISED ON A SMALL PLINTH, HAS VARYING OPACITIES OF GLASS TO ENHANCE PRIVACY—FROM TRANSPARENT ON THE GROUND FLOOR TO TRANSLUCENT ON THE UPPER FLOOR.

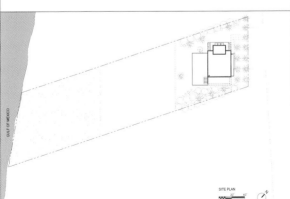

↑ COLUMNS THREAD FROM ONE FLOOR TO THE NEXT, INDEPENDENT OF THE WALLS, MAKING POSSIBLE THE CURTAIN WALLS THAT OPEN THE INTERIORS TO DRAMATIC VIEWS.

← SITE PLAN.

SITE PLAN

BIRD KEY HOUSE, 2004

Sarasota, Florida

This 4,800-square-foot residence on Sarasota Bay was elevated to meet flood codes. The living spaces float above the belly of the house, which serves as a circulation corridor from front to back. The bay side of the home is more transparent. Effecting a Miesian move, Peterson placed the structure on a privacy wall that wraps around to form a courtyard.

→ THE LARGE RECTANGLE THAT ENVELOPS THE STRUCTURE WAS PUSHED, PULLED, AND ERODED AWAY IN A PLAY OF SIMPLE GEOMETRY UNTIL THE BUILDING BECAME A SERIES OF MASSES HELD WITHIN AN OUTER PAVILION.

↓ THIS VIEW OF THE HOUSE ILLUSTRATES THE PRECISION OF PETERSON'S
GEOMETRY, AS THE VOLUMES ARE OPPOSITES IN THEIR TRANSPARENCY AND
OPAQUENESS BUT BOUND IN A RIGOROUS HARMONY.

↓ THE PROTRUDING RECTANGLE HOLDS THE FAMILY ROOM AND ACTS AS A TERRACE FOR THE BEDROOM ABOVE. PETERSON PERFORATED THE ROOF TO OPEN THE ADJACENT INTERIOR SPACE TO LIGHT.

→ BENEATH THE HOUSE, CONCRETE EMBEDDED WITH SHELLS FRAMES WATER FEATURES. THE ROLLED EDGES OF THE MATERIAL EXEMPLIFY PETERSON'S ATTENTION TO DETAIL.

1 bedroom
2 guest suite
3 covered terrace

1 living room
2 dining room
3 kitchen
4 master bedroom
5 master bathroom
6 theater
7 covered terrace

1 foyer
2 garage
3 deck
4 pool
5 reflective pool

↑ THIS VIEW ILLUSTRATES THE TRANSPARENCY OF THE INTERIORS:
ONE SPACE FLOWS INTO THE NEXT, SUBTLY SEPARATED BY VARYING
CEILING PLANES.

→ GROUND, FIRST-FLOOR, AND SECOND-FLOOR PLANS.

↑ A PERFECT EXAMPLE OF PETERSON'S ABILITY TO CREATE SURPRISE IS THE GLASS FLOOR BENEATH THE STAIRS, WHICH OPENS THE VIEW FROM THE STAIRS TO THE BELLY OF THE HOUSE. A MIX OF TRANSPARENT AND TRANSLUCENT SAND-BLASTED GLASS HEIGHTENS PRIVACY.

SANDERLING BEACH HOUSE #2, 2004

Sarasota, Florida

This residence is a work in progress that brought Peterson an Unbuilt Award from the Gulf Coast Chapter of the AIA. An internal blue box, covered in one-inch-by-one-inch tiles, is solid as it thrusts through the roof and broken as it reaches downward beneath the main massing, creating the illusion that the design is a building within a building.

↓ A SKETCH OF THE SITE, WHICH IS BOUNDED ON TWO SIDES BY WATER.

→ VARIED WINDOW PATTERNS ARE FRAMED BY COMMANDING SHADOW-BOX PAVILIONS IN VARYING SHAPES AND SIZES.

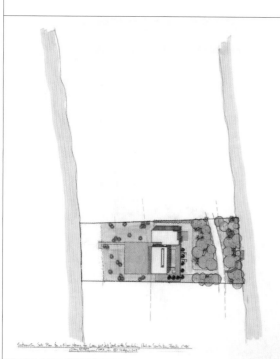

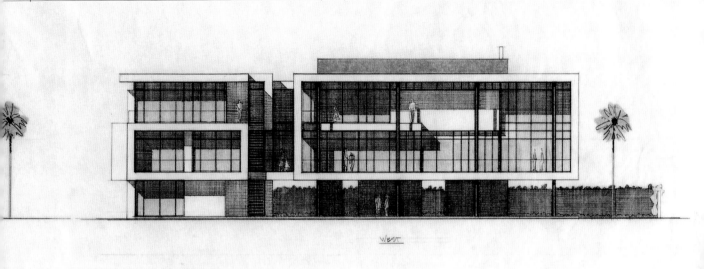

WEST

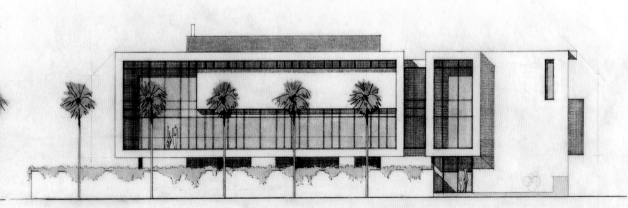

EAST

and Jeff Steele in the Sanderling Club on Siesta Key, Florida. Schematic Elevations @ 1/8"=1'-0"
Guy Peterson /OFA, Inc @ 3.18.05

GIRL SCOUTS OF GULFCOAST FLORIDA, 2005

Sarasota, Florida

This project, a competitive selection that Peterson's firm was awarded, consists of an administration building and program-training center for the Girl Scouts. With a combined 27,000 square feet of built space, the two buildings are connected by a boardwalk that meanders through six of twelve acres of wetlands. The architecture of these buildings is more forceful than the ubiquitous cabinlike architecture generally associated with scout groups, though it is no less at home in the wild, natural setting.

→ PETERSON DESIGNED A GRID SYSTEM FOR THE WINDOWED WALL. THE INSPIRATION WAS A MONDRIAN PAINTING.

↓ AS THE VIEWER APPROACHES THE BUILDINGS, THE DARK SLOPING VOLUMES SEEM FINLIKE AS THEY RISE SKYWARD.

↓↓ ONE OF TWO SLOPING "TUBES" WRAPPED IN A SHEATH OF BLACK METAL THAT FLANK A SERIES OF CONTRASTING VOLUMES IN PRISTINE WHITE.

↓ THE ELONGATED LIGHT PATTERNS THAT FLOW INTO THE INTERIORS ARE EXCELLENT EXAMPLES OF PETERSON'S ABILITY TO CREATE MOMENTS OF SURPRISE.

↓↓ SITE PLAN.

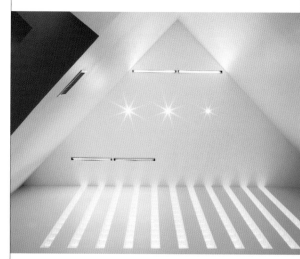

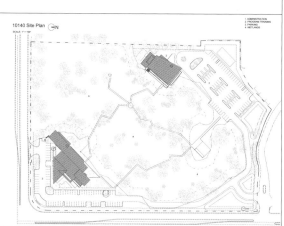

↓ THE ROOF PLANE JUTS OUT OVER THE GRIDDED WINDOW SYSTEM, A MIX OF CLEAR GLASS, SEMI-TRANSLUCENT GLASS, AND ALUMINUM PANELS.

HAWTHORNE STREET HOUSE, 2005

Sarasota, Florida

This client asked Peterson to use very simple, natural materials to reinterpret mid-century modern design precepts. To accomplish this, he chose concrete for floors and plywood for walls. The 2,900-square-foot home, nestled into a traditional neighborhood, has a privacy wall that serves a dual purpose: providing seclusion within the enclosure and creating a linear cohesiveness with the building. The house wraps around the pool, which Peterson made a focal point in the interiors by opening every room to views of the courtyard. The Florida AIA awarded Peterson an Award of Excellence in Architecture for this project.

→ THE ROOF FLOATS OUT OVER THE SHELL OF THE STRUCTURE, AND H-SHAPED I-BEAMS EXPRESS THE STRUCTURAL GRID.

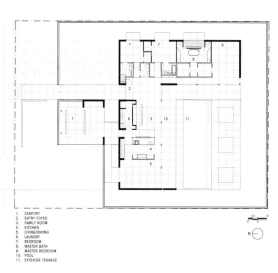

1. CARPORT
2. ENTRY FOYER
3. FAMILY ROOM
4. KITCHEN
5. LIVING/DINING
6. LAUNDRY
7. BEDROOM
8. BEDROOM
9. MASTER BATH
10. MASTER BEDROOM
10. POOL
11. EXTERIOR TERRACE

N

← RECESSES FOR LIGHTING WERE STRATEGICALLY PLACED IN ALL AREAS OF THE INTERIOR TO BATHE THE SPACES IN LIGHT WITHOUT INTERRUPTING THE CLEAN LINES OF THE CEILING PLANE.

↑ HORIZONTALITY IS EXPRESSED IN THE DESIGN. THE STREET-FACING FACADE HAS A ZEN-LIKE SIMPLICITY.

→ FLOOR PLAN.

FERGUSON RESIDENCE, 2005

Englewood, Florida

This 4,066-square-foot beachfront home on Manasota Key is sited on a piece of property with an abundance of native trees. Peterson placed the living and master bedroom spaces on the third floor to open them to the best views. The home is arranged within three vaults that create dramatic drumlike forms on the roof. The ocular opening to the right protrudes from the dining area, while the one to the left is adjacent to the kitchen. Rising between the two is a three-story foyer. A third vault—angling away from the others—holds the master bedroom suite. The minimal trim in the interiors is a hallmark of Peterson's refined design vocabulary.

→ THE ROUND ELEMENTS OF THE DESIGN EMPHASIZE THE UPPER VOLUMES, WHICH RISE ABOVE THE TREETOPS.

↑ THE HOOK-BACK APPROACH TO THE HOME REQUIRES WINDING TOWARD THE STRUCTURE, A SLEIGHT-OF-HAND THAT PETERSON EMPLOYS TO PROVIDE SEQUENTIAL ENTRANCE EXPERIENCES.

↑ THE ANGLED PAVILION TO THE FAR LEFT IS THE MASTER BEDROOM SUITE.

↑ THE ROOM'S TRANSPARENCY MAKES THE VIEW OF THE GULF OF MEXICO
THROUGH THE GLASS WALL SEPARATING THE MASTER BATHROOM FROM THE
MASTER BEDROOM MORE DRAMATIC.

↑ THE MASTER BEDROOM VAULT IN THE DISTANCE IS SLANTED AWAY TO PROVIDE THE HOMEOWNERS WITH PRIVACY AND TO OPEN THE VIEWS OF THE GULF FROM THE OTHER BALCONIES.

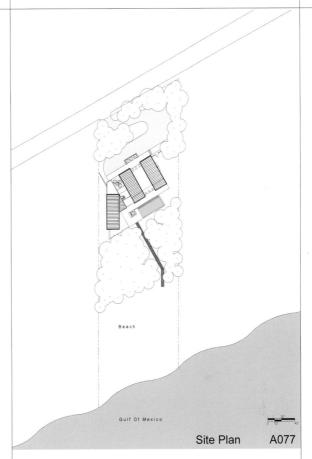

Beach

Gulf Of Mexico

Site Plan   A077

↑ SITE PLAN.

1234 FIRST STREET (2011 projected)

Sarasota, Florida

This study for a mixed-use development for downtown Sarasota introduces four two-story units within a ten-story condominium building that has a rooftop common area inset with a pool.

↓ IN THE SOUTH ELEVATION, A WINDOWED PUNCTURE IN THE UPPER MASSING OF THE BUILDING ALLOWS SWIMMERS TO TAKE IN THE VIEW FROM THE POOL.

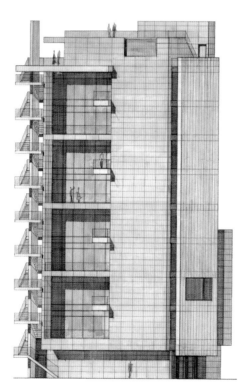

South Elevation

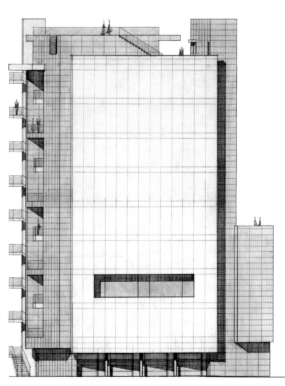

East Elevation

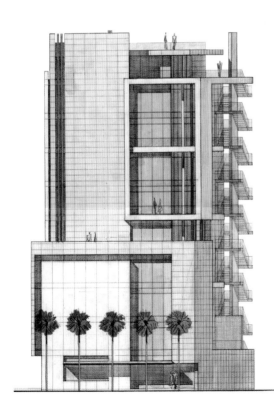

North Elevation

West Elevation

ALBERTO ALFONSO, AIA

Alberto Alfonso is a founding principal and president of Alfonso Architects, an award-winning architectural firm in Tampa, Florida. Mr. Alfonso received the Eduardo Garcia Award for Young Architects in 1987, and under his leadership Alfonso Architects, Inc., received the Firm of the Year award from the Florida Association of the AIA in 2003 and the Firm of the Year award from the Tampa Bay AIA in 2007.

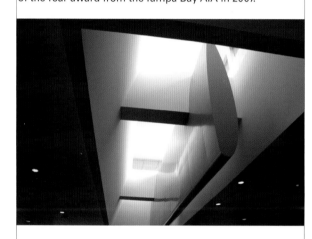

Most recently, Mr. Alfonso was awarded the prestigious Florida Association of the AIA Design Honor in 2008. This award was given in recognition of the high quality and originality of his work over an extended period of time, for advancing the cause and public value of architecture in Florida, and for the leadership and inspiration he provides to his colleagues.

Recent projects recognized by the Florida State AIA Design Awards program include Tampa International Airport's Airside C (a 110,000-square-foot airside serving Southwest Airlines), Nielsen Media Research Global Technology Center (a 650,000-square-foot corporate campus headquarters), the Mission of St. Mary Chapel, the University of South Florida School of Psychology/Communication Sciences & Disorders Building, and the Sam Rampello Downtown Partnership K–8 School.

Mr. Alfonso is currently a member of the American Institute of Architects, a USF Graphic Studio board member, a member of the Florida Communities Trust, and a member of the Professional Liaison Committee of the University of Florida School of Architecture. He has also served on Tampa's Architectural Review Committee and the Ybor City Barrio Latino Commission.

Mr. Alfonso resides in Tampa with his wife and their two children.

RENÉ GONZÁLEZ, AIA

Principal of René González Architect, René González served as project designer with architect Richard Meier on the Getty Museum and Center in Los Angeles, and has collaborated with Frank Israel. In Florida, other internationally recognized collaborations and projects include the Wolfsonian Museum with Mark Hampton, FAIA. He has designed and curated museum and gallery installations for various institutions, including the Cisneros Fontanals Art Foundation, the Miami Art Museum, the Museum of Contemporary Art in Miami, and the Arango Design Foundation. He has also completed residential projects for numerous art collectors.

Mr. González's work has been published widely in various national and international industry and consumer publications, including the *New York Times, New York, Robb Report, American Airlines Nexos, Architectural Record, Wallpaper, Metropolis, Metropolitan Home, Interior Design, House and Garden, Architectural Digest, Objekt International, Florida International Magazine, Home Miami, Condo Living, Casa & Estilo, Quaderns, Ocean Drive, Florida Inside Out,* and the *Miami Herald.*

He has lectured and taught on architecture, art, and design at UCLA, the University of Virginia, Florida International University, the Universidad San Francisco de Ecuador, and the Universidad Central de Venezuela. His projects have been exhibited at national museums and galleries in Miami, Los Angeles, and Quito, Ecuador.

Among other honors, Mr. González has received an AIA National Honor Award, Excellence in Architecture Awards from AIA Miami, and *Metropolitan Home* magazine's Home of the Year Award for design excellence, and he was recently honored by Conde Nast's *House & Garden* as one of fifty designers who represent the future of design internationally. He has been selected by a jury of the Smithsonian to the Hispanic Design Archive at the Cooper-Hewitt National Design Museum in New York, and has been appointed by the mayor and commissioners of Miami Beach to chair the Miami Beach Design Review Board.

In the Miami community, Mr. González has worked to promote contemporary design and architecture to the general public by coordinating and sponsoring exhibitions and lectures and by serving on boards and committees and as the president of the Arango Design Foundation.

Mr. González holds a master of architecture degree from UCLA and a bachelor of design degree from the University of Florida. He is a member of the American Institute of Architects and a licensed architect in Florida and New York.

CHAD OPPENHEIM, NCARB, AIA

Born in New Hyde Park in 1971 and raised in the suburbs of New Jersey, Mr. Oppenheim received a bachelor of architecture degree from Cornell University in 1994, and founded OPPENHEIM Architecture + Design in 1999. An adjunct professor of architecture at Florida International University, he has lectured globally and is the recipient of numerous awards and distinctions. Mr. Oppenheim lives and works with his wife and muse, Ilona, in Miami.

He has published in the *New York Times*, *Elle Décor*, *House and Garden*, *O At Home*, *Robb Report*, *Town & Country*, the *Wall Street Journal*, *Architectural Digest*, *Robb Report Vacation Homes*, *Wallpaper*, *Condé Nast Portfolio*, *Miami Modern Luxury*, *Wired*, *Casamica*, *Blueprint Directory*, *Florida Inside Out*, *Ocean Drive*, the *Miami Herald Home & Design Magazine*, *Art Basel Miami*, *Surface*, *Miami Home & Décor*, *Estilos de Vida*, *Avenue*, *City Smart*, the *Miami Herald*, and many others.

GUY W. PETERSON, NCARB, FAIA

Guy W. Peterson is a lifetime Sarasota resident. He received his bachelor of design degree in architecture with honors from the University of Florida in 1976, and he went on to earn his master of arts in architecture degree with high honors from the University of Florida Graduate Design Program in 1978. As president and principal architect of Guy Peterson | Office for Architecture, Inc., he directs a wide range of activities for the firm, including overall responsibility for project design.

He is a modernist in his approach, and the language of his architecture is honesty and simplicity. His work is poetic and human; it evokes emotion and comes from the heart. Through his use of color, indigenous materials, and light and shadow, he has derived an aesthetic that results in a clean, sustainable, and delightful architecture.

Since the inception of his practice in 1980, Mr. Peterson has received more than fifty design awards and special recognitions for his work, including thirty-six design awards from the American Institute of Architects. In 1998 he became

Mr. Oppenheim's awards include the Baird Prize, Japan; the Kume Fellowship, Japan; the American Architecture Award, Chicago Athenaeum; AIA Miami's Honorary Outstanding Young Architect of the Year (2001); Midnight Affair Design Excellence Award: Best Outdoor Space (2004); and more than twenty AIA awards for his architectural projects.

Lectures include "Not Your Grandmother's Condominium," Quito Biennale in Quito, Ecuador; "Chad Oppenheim, Architect," Sarasota Design Biennale; "Defining Your Style," the *New York Times* and *Architectural Digest* Home Show in New York; "Waterside Architecture & Design, Connecting with Communities," Cityscape Abu Dhabi Waterfront Development Conference in the United Arab Emirates; and "In Search of Essence," which he presented during the Northern Virginia Chapter of AIA (NOVA) Design Awards in Washington, D.C.

one of the youngest architects in Florida to win the prestigious Award of Honor for Design from the Florida Association of the AIA.

In 2000 he received the Distinguished Architecture Alumnus Award from the University of Florida School of Architecture. In 2003 he became the only architect from Florida to be elected into the College of Fellows of the American Institute of Architects for his notable contributions to the advancement of the profession of architecture. In 2006, the American Jewish Committee honored him with a Civic Achievement Award, and in 2007 he received the Lifetime Achievement Award from the Sarasota Architectural Foundation.

Mr. Peterson belongs to a number of professional and community organizations. He is an active member of the University of Florida School of Architecture, where he serves on the Professional Advisory Committee and as a regular guest juror. He is also a trustee of the Florida Foundation for Architecture, and he is a member of the advisory board of the Sarasota Architectural Foundation, a local organization whose focus is preserving the work of the Sarasota School of Architecture and beyond. Additionally, he is a member of the Sarasota Tiger Bay Club and a founding member of the Sarasota business group Enzyme.

Mr. Peterson has been a guest lecturer on programs at a number of gatherings: Sarasota Architectural Foundation (2007); the Senior Academy on Architecture (2003, 2004, 2007); the American Institute of Architects, AIA Florida, Young Architects Forum (2006); the American Institute of Architects, AIA Southwest Florida Chapter Design Conference (keynote speaker, September 2005); the American Institute of Architects, AIA Southwest Florida Chapter (2002);

the American Institute of Architects, AIA Florida Gulf Coast Chapter, Sarasota Design Conference (2002); the University of Florida School of Architecture ("Journeying Toward Essentialism" lecture, 2002); the American Institute of Architects, AIA Orlando Chapter (2001); the American Legacy Symposium (2001); and the Sarasota County Arts Council (Smartalk, 1997).

Mr. Peterson is a Registered Architect in Florida, Indiana, and Massachusetts, and he holds a certificate from the National Council of Architectural Registration Boards (NCARB).

NOTES

PHOTO CREDITS

PREFACE
1. Le Corbusier, *Towards a New Architecture*, trans. Frederick Etchells (New York: Dover, 1986), 5.
2. Le Corbusier, *Towards a New Architecture*, 1.

CHAPTER 1
1. Michael Leyton, *Symmetry, Causality, Mind* (Cambridge: MIT Press, 1992), 8–9.

CHAPTER 2
1. Paul Ricoeur, "Universal Civilization and National Cultures," in *Architectural Regionalism: Collected Writings on Place, Identity, Modernity and Tradition*, ed. Vincent B. Canizaro (Princeton: Princeton Architectural Press, 2007), 51. The chapter is reprinted from Ricoeur's *History and Truth*. (Evanston, IL: Northwestern University Press, 1965), 271–84.
2. Le Corbusier, John Goodman, and Jean-Louis Cohen, *Toward an Architecture* (London: Frances Lincoln, 2008), 100.

CHAPTER 3
1. Colin Rowe, *The Mathematics of the Ideal Villa and Other Essays* (Cambridge, MA: MIT Press, 1982), 1–27.
2. Le Corbusier, *Toward an Architecture*, trans. Frederick Etchells (London: John Rodker, 1931), 29.

CHAPTER 4
1. Roberto de Alba, *Paul Rudolph: The Late Work* (New York: Princeton Architectural Press, 2003), 203.
2. John Howey, FAIA. Personal correspondence, April 1, 2008.

CHAPTER 1
p. 18: Al Hurley
p. 21: No credit
p. 23: Al Hurley
p. 24 and 25: Al Hurley
p. 26: George Cott
p. 27: Al Hurley
p. 28: No credit
p. 29: No credit
p. 30: Al Hurley
pp. 32–33: Al Hurley
p. 33: Alfonso Architects
p. 34: Al Hurley
p. 34, bottom: Alfonso Architects
p. 35, top left and right: Al Hurley
pp. 36–39: Al Hurley
p. 40–41: George Cott
p. 42: George Cott
p. 42–43: Alfonso Architects
p. 43: Al Hurley
p. 44: Al Hurley
p. 45: George Cott
p. 46–47: Al Hurley
pp. 48–49: George Cott
p. 50, top: George Cott
p. 51: George Cott
p. 52: George Cott
p. 53, top left: Al Hurley
p. 53, top right: Alfonso Architects
p. 53, bottom: George Cott
p. 54–55: Alfonso Architects
p. 56: all Al Hurley
p. 57, top: Al Hurley
p. 57, bottom left and right: Alfonso Architects
p. 58, bottom left and right: Al Hurley
pp. 58–59, top: Alfonso Architects
pp. 60–61: Al Hurley
p. 62–63: Alfonso Architects
pp. 64–67: Al Hurley
p. 68, bottom: Alfonso Architects
p. 68, top left & right; page 69: Al Hurley
p. 70, left: Alfonso Architects
p. 70, right: 71: Al Hurley
p. 72: Al Hurley
p. 73, top left: Al Hurley
p. 73, bottom left: Alfonso Architects
p. 73, far right: Alfonso Architects
p. 74, left and right: Al Hurley
p. 75: Al Hurley
p. 76–77: Al Hurley
p. 78–79: Alfonso Architects
pp. 80–81: Alfonso Architects
pp. 82–85: Al Hurley
pp. 86–87: Alfonso Architects

CHAPTER 2
p. 88: Marcelo Aniello
p. 91: Ken Hayden
p. 92: René González Architect, Inc.
p. 93: Hikari Studio & Rene Gonzalez Architect, Inc.
p. 95, top: Oriol Tarridas
p. 95, bottom: Hikari Studio
p. 97: No credit
p. 98: Monica Vazquez
p. 101, left: Steven Brooke Studio
p. 101, right: René González Architect, Inc.
pp. 102–111: Rene Gonzalez Architect, Inc.
p. 112, top: Ken Hayden
p. 112, bottom: René González Architect, Inc.
p. 113: Ken Hayden
p. 114, top right, middle, and left: Ken Hayden
p. 114, bottom: Jose Zaldivar
pp. 115–117: Ken Hayden
pp. 118–119: Oriol Tarridas
p. 120, top: Monica Vazquez
p. 120, bottom: Massimo Listri
p. 121: Oriol Tarridas
p. 122, bottom: Massimo Listri
p. 122, top: René González Architect, Inc.
p. 123: Oriol Tarridas
pp. 124–125: Steven Brooke Studio
p. 126, bottom and top left: Steven Brooke Studio
p. 126, bottom and top right: René González Architect, Inc.
p. 127: Steven Brooke Studio
p. 128, left: Hikari Studio & René González Architect, Inc.
p. 128–129: Curtis Woodhouse
p. 130: Hikari Studio & René González Architect, Inc.
p. 131: René González Architect, Inc.
pp. 132–134: Spine 3-D
p. 135: René González Architect, Inc.
p. 136: No credit
p. 137: Hikari Studio
p. 138, top: No credit
p. 138, bottom: Hikari Studio
p. 139: Hikari Studio
p. 140, top, middle, and bottom: René González Architect, Inc.
p. 140–141: Hikari Studio
pp. 142–145, left: Render Solutions
pp. 145–147: René González Architect, Inc.

CHAPTER 3

p. 148: Rodrigo Londono
p. 151: Ken Hayden
p. 153, top: dbox
p. 153, bottom left: Oppenheim Architecture + Design
p. 153, bottom right: Eric Laignel
p. 155: Olalekan Jeyifous
p. 156, left: dbox
p. 156, right: Oppenheim Architecture + Design
p. 159: Cicada Design, Inc.
pp. 160–161: Vyonyx
pp. 164–169: Eric Laignel
p. 170–171: Ken Hayden
p. 172, bottom left: Oppenheim Architecture + Design
pp. 172, top left, top right, and bottom right: Ken Hayden
p. 173, top: Oppenheim Architecture + Design
p. 173, bottom: Ken Hayden
pp. 174–177: Oppenheim Architecture + Design
pp. 178–182: Ken Hayden
pp. 183–191: Oppenheim Architecture + Design
p. 192: Totus Photography
p. 193, bottom left: Oppenheim Architecture + Design
p. 193, bottom right: Ken Hayden
p. 193, top: dbox
p. 194, left: Robin Hill
p. 194–195: Oppenheim Architecture + Design
p. 196, left: Oppenheim Architecture + Design
p. 196–198: dbox
p. 199, right: dbox
p. 199, left top, middle, and right: Oppenheim Architecture + Design
pp. 200–201: dbox
p. 202, left: Oppenheim Architecture + Design
pp. 202, right–205: dbox
pp. 206–209: dbox
pp. 210– 213

CHAPTER 4

p. 214: Barbara Banks
pp. 217–223: Steven Brooke Studio
p. 225: Guy Peterson OFA
pp. 229, 230: Steven Traves
pp. 227–231: Steven Brooke Studio
p. 232: Guy Peterson OFA
pp. 233–240: Steven Brooke Studio
p. 241, top: Guy Peterson OFA
p. 241, bottom–243, top: Steven Brooke Studio
p. 243, bottom: P. Rudolph and R. Twitchell
pp. 244–255, left: Steven Brooke Studio
p. 255, right: Guy Peterson OFA
pp. 256–261, left: Steven Brooke Studio
p. 261, right: Guy Peterson OFA
pp. 262–266: Steven Brooke Studio
p. 267: Guy Peterson OFA
pp. 268–271: Steven Brooke Studio
pp. 272–277, top: Steven Brooke Studio
p. 277, bottom: Guy Peterson OFA
pp. 278–282, left: Steven Brooke Studio
p. 282, right: Guy Peterson OFA
p. 283: Steven Brooke Studio
pp. 284–285: Guy Peterson OFA
pp. 286–288, top right: Steven Brooke Studio
p. 288, bottom right: Guy Peterson OFA
p. 289: Steven Brooke Studio
pp. 290–293, top: Steven Brooke Studio
p. 293, bottom: Guy Peterson OFA
pp. 294–299, left: Steven Brooke Studio
p. 299, right: Guy Peterson OFA
pp. 300–301: Guy Peterson OFA

BACKMATTER

p. 302: Al Hurley
p. 303: Daniel Romero
p. 304: Oppenheim Architecture + Design
p. 305: Steven Brooke Studio